ENCYCLOPEDIA OF MAMMALS

VOLUME 15
Tig–Wha

MARSHALL CAVENDISH
NEW YORK • LONDON • TORONTO • SYDNEY

TIGERS

RELATIONS

The tiger belongs to the cat family, Felidae, and the order Carnivora. Other members of this family include:

LEOPARDS

JAGUAR

LIONS

CHEETAHS

PUMAS

OCELOT

LYNX

A. & M. Shah/Planet Earth Pictures

THE ULTIMATE PREDATOR

THE STRIKINGLY STRIPED COAT OF THE MAGNIFICENT TIGER AFFORDS NEAR-PERFECT CAMOUFLAGE IN THE DENSE UNDERGROWTH OF ITS JUNGLE HOME

T he tiger is the biggest of all the living cats. It lives by stealth, silently stalking its prey through the dense under-growth of its jungle home.

Like all cats, the tiger is a meat-eater, or carni-vore, so it hunts and kills other animals for its food. Its strikingly striped coat offers it great camouflage in the long grasses in which it hunts, particularly at dusk when the setting sun and long shadows make it especially difficult to see.

Like most hunters that are active at night, the tiger has excellent vision. Its highly developed eyesight is so acute that it can detect even the smallest movement of its intended prey. It is able to magnify dull rays of light through its pupils. This means that its vision is sharp, even in the darkest hours of night. This keen eyesight is aided by an exceptionally acute sense of hearing.

The tiger as we know it today probably evolved in the cold northern forests of Siberia. It started

CLASSIFICATION

Tigers are meat-eaters, or carnivores, and belong to the catlike group. All tigers belong to the same genus and species, but there were eight sub-species, or different kinds. The five living sub-species are listed below

ORDER
Carnivora
(carnivores)

SUPERFAMILY
Feloidea
(catlike forms)

FAMILY
Felidae
(cats)

GENUS
Panthera

SPECIES
tigris

SUBSPECIES
P. t. tigris
(Bengal tiger)

P. t. altaica
(Siberian tiger)

P. t. amoyensis
(South China tiger)

P. t. corbetti
(Indochinese tiger)

P. t. sumatrae
(Sumatran tiger)

spreading throughout Asia about two million years ago, during the Quaternary period. Its ancestry can be traced back to the small animal that is the ancestor of all modern cats, including the domestic cat. Known as *Dinictis* (*DIN-ick-tis*), this cat had a long body and sharp, pointed teeth called canines. It lived about 36 million years ago and gave rise to two lines of cats (see box on page 2164).

No one knows for sure how tigers spread out to reach their present homes, but it is thought that worsening weather conditions in Siberia forced them to move south. Once they reached warmer habitats, they spread to the east and west until they reached impassable barriers such as the vast mountain range of the Himalayas and the Gobi desert.

THE TIGER IS A TERRITORIAL AND SOLITARY ANIMAL. IF TWO MEET UNEXPECTEDLY, THEY MAY FIGHT

Some tigers headed into Manchuria and Korea, while others reached Turkestan and, eventually, India. It is interesting to note that there are no tigers in Sri Lanka, which suggests that they did not arrive in India until after that island separated from the mainland. The tigers settled into the lush Indian forests and their numbers grew dramatically. They continued to spread eastward, reaching China, Indochina and the Malay Peninsula. Some even managed to cross the sea to Sumatra, then moved into Java and Bali. From there the sea was too wide for even this accomplished swimmer; consequently there are no tigers in Borneo or Sulawesi.

Tigers in different areas developed different

A young tiger (above) *exploring outside its den. It will stay with its mother for about two years.*

WHITE TIGERS

White tigers have been seen in many parts of India. Some are true albinos (animals, including humans, that are born without the coloring pigment in their skin or hair). They have pure white coats and characteristic pink eyes. But others have an eggshell-white or cream-colored coat with brown or black stripes. These tigers also have striking, ice-blue eyes.

Many of these tigers were found in the Rewa district of northern India. Native princes regarded white tigers as rarities, and prize specimens were kept in private zoos. In the 1920s when one white tiger died, it was stuffed and sent to the emperor, King George V of England.

characteristics, which led to their being classified as different subspecies. Of these, the Siberian tiger (*Panthera tigris altaica*), found in the forests of Siberia, is the largest of all living cats, measuring up to 13 ft (4 m) long and weighing about 617 lb (280 kg). It has a massive head, long fur, and stocky hind legs. Its thick coat is reddish yellow—usually lighter than the coats of other tigers—with large black stripes. It also tends to have a higher proportion of white on its coat, helping it blend into the snowy background. Its large, bulky body and thick coat are adaptations to life in the cold, where temperatures can drop to -31°F (-35°C). Siberian tigers

The coat markings of a tiger are stunning.

Unfortunately, this has meant death to many of them.

Gerard Lacz/NHPA

Planet Earth Pictures

are greatly threatened with extinction. It is believed that there are only about four hundred of these magnificent animals left in the wild.

The Caspian tiger (*P. t. virgata*), Javan tiger (*P. t. sondaica*), and the Bali tiger (*P. t. balica*) are all now extinct. The Bengal or Indian tiger (*P. t. tigris*) is by far the most numerous of the existing tigers, with a total population of some three thousand. It lives in India and the mangrove forests of the Sundarbans in east India and Bangladesh, as well as in Burma and parts of Nepal.

The South China tiger (*P. t. amoyensis*) is small-er than the Bengal tiger. It has a smooth coat with short, broad black stripes and very little white. It was once common throughout eastern China, but nowadays sightings are exceedingly rare. Not more than a couple dozen still exist in the wild; they live in the Yangtze Valley of Szechwan.

The Indochinese or Malayan tiger (*P. t. corbetti*) is slimmer and smaller than the South China tiger. It was once common throughout southern China, Vietnam, Laos, Malaysia, and Burma. Nowadays it numbers just over one thousand and is found in the jungles of Malaysia, Thailand, Burma, and much of Indochina.

The Javan tiger, Sumatran tiger (*P. t. sumatrae*), and the Bali tiger probably all descended from the Indochinese tiger. These tigers are comparatively small, measuring less than 10 ft (3 m) long. ■

THE TIGERS' FAMILY TREE

This family tree shows how all the different subspecies of tigers are related to each other and to other members of the cat family.
The tiger's closest relatives are the other
members of the genus Panthera: *the lion, jaguar, and leopard.*

LEOPARD
Panthera pardus
(*pan-THARE-a par-dus*)

LION
Panthera leo
(*pan-THARE-a LEE-o*)

JAGUAR
Panthera onca (*pan-THARE-a ON-ka*)

ANCESTORS

The tiger's early ancestor gave rise to two lines of cats—the stabbing cats and the biting cats. The stabbing cats were among the largest and most powerful predators of their day. The best known was called *Smilodon* (**SMILE-o-don**) or the saber-toothed tiger. Its most striking feature was its enormous canine teeth, which were up to 6 in (15 cm) long and curved backward. Because it had weak jaws, it used these to stab its prey, hacking into the neck region, then retreating as the animal bled to death. All stabbing cats are extinct today.

Although *Smilodon* is called the saber-toothed tiger, it is only distantly related to the tiger of today. Tigers evolved from the second evolutionary line, the biting cats. Unlike the stabbing cats, biting cats have powerful jaws and kill their prey by hooking the canines in the flesh, then snapping the neck or strangling the prey.

The canines are vital to the tiger. Should it lose them, it would have nothing with which to grab prey, and it would then eventually starve to death.

Illustrations by Peter David Scott/Wildlife Art Agency

TIGER

Panthera tigris
(pan-THARE-a TIG-ris)

Closely related to the tiger are the other big cats in the Panthera genus. Also classed as big cats are the cheetah and the clouded leopard. Through the millions of years of evolution and migration, tigers evolved characteristics that helped them adapt to their different regions. Recognized in eight regions, these differences are so marked that the tigers are classified as different subspecies. Most tigers spend their lives within a set territory, and it is these territorial habits that are thought to have led to the spread of the tiger throughout Asia from the north. As their numbers grew, they needed more land, so they continued to move farther south.

Other relatives of the tiger include the small cats from the genus Felis. There are thirty species of small cats, including the ocelot (Felis pardalis), the puma (F. concolor), the lynx (F. lynx), and the wildcat (F. sylvestris), which includes the domestic cat.

Of the thirty species of small cats, ten are found only in the New World, eighteen are found only in the Old World, the lynx is found in both, and the domestic cat is now worldwide.

BIG CATS

SMALL CATS

OCELOT

ALL CATS

ANATOMY:
THE TIGER

THE HEAD

The tiger's head is foreshortened and powerfully constructed. It measures about 14 in (35 cm) long. The strong bones are designed to absorb the stress of its powerful killing bite.

THE TIGER'S COAT

gives it excellent camouflage in the dappled light of evening and dawn. The stripes also break up the outline of the big cat, making it harder to see against the long grasses through which it stalks its prey.

The largest species of tigers is the male Siberian tiger (see Fact File box). It is the world's largest living cat. The smallest tiger is the Sumatran tiger. Females are smaller than males.

EARS

The tiger has very good hearing. The rounded ear flaps funnel sounds into the inner ear.

FORELEGS

and shoulders are heavily muscled and very powerful. They have long, sharp, retractable claws, measuring up to 2.5 in (6 cm) long. Each forepaw has five claws, while the rear paws have only four. The claws enable the tiger to grab on to its prey.

SOFT FOOTPADS

enable it to pick its way silently across the forest floor. Because the paws are so sensitive, tigers find it difficult to walk on sharp or hot surfaces.

Illustrations Matthew Hillier/Wildlife Art Agency

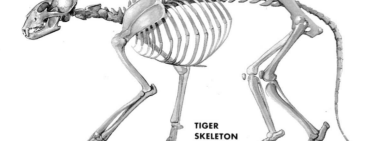

TIGER SKELETON

The hyoid bone, or tongue bone, of a small cat enables it to purr continuously. Small cats cannot roar.

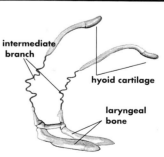

SMALL CAT'S TONGUE BONE

intermediate branch

hyoid cartilage

laryngeal bone

Tigers have a small piece of cartilage at the base of their tongues (above), which enables them to roar when they breathe out, but not purr.

X-ray illustrations Gary Martin/Wildlife Art Agency

SUMATRAN　　　**SIBERIAN**　　　**WHITE TIGER**

Illustration Matthew Hillier/Wildlife Art Agency

FACT FILE:

SIBERIAN TIGER

CLASSIFICATION

GENUS: *PANTHERA*

SPECIES: *TIGRIS*　　SUBSPECIES: *ALTAICA*

SIZE

HEAD-BODY LENGTH/MALE: 106–150 IN (270–380 CM). FEMALES ARE SMALLER

SHOULDER HEIGHT/MALE: 41–43 IN (105–110 CM)

TAIL LENGTH: 39 IN (100 CM)

WEIGHT: 550–675 LB (250–306 KG)

WEIGHT AT BIRTH: 27–53 OZ (785–1,500 G)

COLORATION

REDDISH GOLDEN COAT WITH BLACK STRIPES

WHITE UNDERSIDE

BENGAL TIGER

CLASSIFICATION

GENUS: *PANTHERA*

SPECIES: *TIGRIS*

SUBSPECIES: *TIGRIS*

SIZE

HEAD-BODY LENGTH/MALE: 74–87 IN (189–220 CM)

SHOULDER HEIGHT/MALE: 35–37 IN (90–95 CM)

TAIL LENGTH: 32–35 IN (81–90 CM)

WEIGHT: 400–575 LB (180–260 KG)

WEIGHT AT BIRTH: 33–42 OZ (925–1,195 G)

COLORATION

COAT IS USUALLY FAWN TO ORANGY RED, WITH LIGHTER FUR ON ITS BELLY

DARK STRIPES

The tiger's teeth are well adapted to killing. The long canines, which can be up to 5 in (13 cm) long, pierce the flesh of the prey, allowing the tiger to secure a firm hold. The carnassials are used to slice through the muscles and tendons of the prey.
Similar to the blades on a pair of scissors, these teeth are ideal for this purpose. The shape and length of the tiger's skull add to the leverage of its jaws, making it difficult for prey to wriggle free.

canine teeth

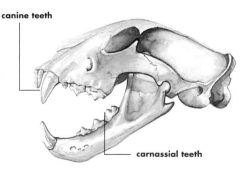

carnassial teeth

SECRETIVE STALKERS

THE SOLITARY AND SECRETIVE TIGER IS MOST ACTIVE DURING THE DIM LIGHTS OF DAWN AND DUSK, USUALLY OPERATING UNDER DENSE COVER

L ittle is known about the habits of the tiger in the wild. The few studies that have been conducted have been focused on the most common of the existing tigers, the Bengal tiger.

Unlike the lion, the tiger is rarely found in open spaces. Its best chance of successful hunting is by stalking its prey and then ambushing it. Its bright reddish gold coat stands out clearly in the starkness of open spaces, but in the dense jungle or under-growth surrounding a water hole, it blends in with the background, becoming almost invisible.

Although tigers are solitary animals and do not usually share their territories, they have been seen to meet casually, without confrontation, and will occasionally share a kill. Male tigers tend to be

A tiger slinks silently and cautiously through the dense undergrowth in search of prey.

A tiger marks his territory by spraying urine at tiger-head height so that other tigers cannot fail to notice he is around.

Anup Shah/Planet Earth Pictures

A tiger sharpens its claws on a tree trunk, leaving a territorial mark at the same time.

more territorial, tolerating transient females more easily than other males. Females share their territories more readily with both males and females.

Tigers mark their territories by scratching trees; spraying a mixture of urine and a secretion from their anal glands on trees, rocks, or bushes along their trails; or leaving a pile of feces in a conspicuous place. This information tells intruders about the resident tiger and also alerts male tigers to females in heat.

TIGERS REGULARLY PATROL THEIR TERRITORIES BECAUSE THEIR SCENT MARKINGS LAST ONLY A FEW HOURS

Like all large predators, the tiger spends much of its time conserving its energy for hunting. Up to 80 percent of its time is spent resting or sleeping. Dawn and dusk often find the tiger grooming itself, licking its fur as domestic cats do.

Tigers usually hunt at night, hiding in the long grasses and sneaking up on their prey in the cover of darkness. They may walk long distances, often along streambeds, paths, or even roads. When the tiger finds its prey, it slinks forward, holding its body low to the ground to avoid detection. The stripes on its coat help break up its telltale outline by matching the shadows cast by the long grasses. ■

HABITATS

ZEFA

her on the hunt, she must be able to find food close to her den so that she can suckle them at regular intervals. When the cubs are a little older, she can travel farther afield, but she must be able to find enough food to feed both herself and her growing brood.

A male tiger's range is usually three or four times bigger than a female's and overlaps the territories of several females so that he can father cubs. Tigers are renowned for their wandering, and each territory will have several dens or sheltered resting places in it. The tiger uses whichever one is most convenient at the time.

Bengal tigers live in all types of forests, including the wet, evergreen, and semievergreen forests of Assam and eastern Bengal; the mangrove forests of the Ganges Delta; the moist deciduous forests of Nepal; and the thorn forests of the Western Ghats.

(Left) *The Siberian tiger's coat is lighter than that of other tigers, which suits its local habitat.*

Typical tiger country has three main features: It will always have good cover, allowing the tiger to stalk its prey without being seen; it will always be close to water; and it will always have plenty of prey animals on which the tiger can feed. Within such country, tigers mark out and operate within individual territories.

The importance of the territory is particularly relevant to the female. If she is familiar with an area, she can be reasonably certain of killing prey with some regularity, allowing her to raise young.. When her cubs are very young and cannot follow

SWIMMING TIGERS

Unlike other cats, which tend to avoid water, tigers actively seek it out. During the extreme heat of the day, they are often found cooling off in pools. Tigers are excellent swimmers, capable of swimming up to four miles (six kilometers), and can even carry their dead prey across water.

It has happened that sleeping fishermen have been killed by tigers. The unfortunate victims had anchored their open boats some distance from the shore, but a boat has to be far out to be beyond a tiger's range.

DISTRIBUTION

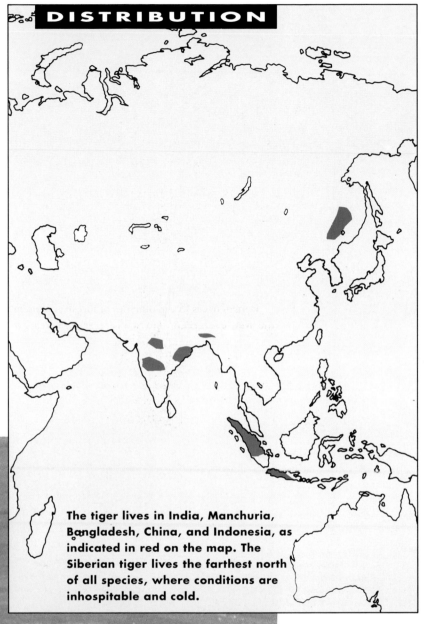

The tiger lives in India, Manchuria, Bangladesh, China, and Indonesia, as indicated in red on the map. The Siberian tiger lives the farthest north of all species, where conditions are inhospitable and cold.

They are also equally at home in heavy grass jungles, bamboo thickets, swamps, and scrubland, which has plenty of cover. Their priorities are water and enough cover to allow them to hunt effectively.

In Burma the tiger is often found in thick forests, while the Indonesian tigers favor dark, humid rain forests. Siberian tigers roam the Amur Basin, preferring the mountain forests, which are not inhabited by humans. Here temperatures can fall to as low as -31°F (-35°C), and there is much snow covering the ground. At this time of year, the Siberian tiger develops an insulating layer of fat on its belly and flanks.

Unlike lions and leopards, tigers do not habitually climb trees; however, females and cubs have displayed considerable climbing abilities when escaping from wild dogs called dholes. Dholes hunt in packs of about thirty, and although the dogs are much smaller than tigers, packs have been seen attacking them.

THE SIBERIAN TIGER OFTEN HAS TO TRAVEL GREAT DISTANCES TO FIND FOOD

Tigers are much stronger than dholes. They are capable of smashing a dhole's skull with just a single swipe from their enormous forepaws. But dholes hunt in packs, nipping the cat's flanks and hindquarters and diverting its attention. Such battles are usually ferocious and noisy. The tiger will inflict heavy casualties on the pack, sometimes killing as many as ten or twelve dogs, before being killed itself. A pack of dholes will also chase a fully grown tiger away from its fresh kill.

Unlike most cats, the tiger loves water, and

KEY FACTS

● When tigers enter the water they often go in backward so that they can keep a watchful eye on their surroundings.

● A tiger's roar can be heard up to 1.5 mi (2.4 km) away.

● A tiger kills the equivalent of 30 buffalo a year. The Siberian tiger needs between 19 and 22 lb (9 and 10 kg) of meat a day.

● It is estimated that more than half of all tiger cubs die before they reach maturity.

● A tiger's nighttime vision is six times better than a human's.

ZEFA

in hot weather it is often seen splashing around in streams and rivers. It is an excellent swimmer capable of long distances. It will even chase prey across a pool, catch it, and swim back to shore with the animal in its mouth. This demonstrates the tiger's remarkable strength: A single tiger can pull a male water buffalo weighing about 2,000 lb (908 kg) to a quiet spot in which to feast. It would take thirteen humans to move such a weight.

Tigers are opportunist hunters. This means they will attack and eat almost any vertebrate animal. Their diet consists mainly of deer such as sambar and chital, wild pigs, birds, monkeys, and even fish, frogs, and lizards. A wounded, elderly, or sick tiger will attack easy targets such as cattle and livestock, and in some instances it has even been known to attack humans.

COMMUNICATION

Tigers have a variety of methods of communication within their territories. They regularly spray bushes and trees with a mixture of urine and anal gland secretions and scratch tree trunks. Both of these marks alert other tigers to their presence.

Tigers also have a wide range of vocal calls, and their roars can travel far. Calling is used to invite other tigers to mate. Sometimes female tigers call

FOCUS ON

THE SUNDARBANS TIGER RESERVE

The Sundarbans Tiger Reserve stretches from West Bengal east to Bangladesh. The world's largest mangrove swamp, it has the largest tiger population of any tiger reserve in India. The maze of narrow channels and the lush vegetation provide plenty of cover; proximity to water and a bountiful supply of prey animals ensure that hunting is good.

Sundarbans is an area of low islets and estuarine swampland situated in the Ganges Delta. It covers an area of some 998 square miles (2,585 square kilometers). The land seldom rises much above sea level. Cyclones and tidal waves regularly occur. Like all predators, tigers play an important role. By killing deer and other prey animals, they help keep the numbers of these animals under control. Most of their prey are herbivores (plant-eaters), and, without some control, they would quickly eat all the vegetation, leaving the area unable to sustain any life.

Sundarbans is home to many other animals, including the estuarine crocodile and the olive ridley sea turtle, both of which are endangered species. Human access across the whole area is restricted, allowing the animals maximum freedom from human molestation.

TEMPERATURE AND RAINFALL

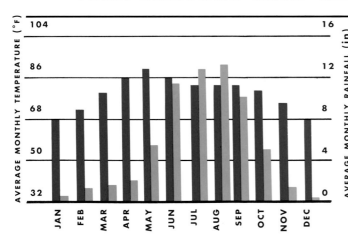

■ TEMPERATURE

■ RAINFALL

Temperatures in the Sundarbans range from 68 to 104°F (20 to 40°C), and there is heavy rainfall during the monsoon months. The area is very flat and is prone to flooding during the rainy season.

their cubs to share a kill but, frequently, roaring, growling, and snarling noises are used to warn other tigers off.

When tigers meet they curl their lips in the *flehmen* reaction (described on page 2178). This is most commonly used when a male and female tiger meet. Their tails also tell whether or not a tiger is receptive to another tiger. An excited tiger will lash its tail quickly from side to side. A nervous or tense tiger will keep its tail low, slowly twitching it. ■

NEIGHBORS

These animals all live in the same area as the Bengal tiger. Although they are all predators, they depend on the rich plant growth for their survival.

VULTURE

The tiger hides its catch from bearded and other vultures, which look for easy pickings.

WATER MONITOR

A large, agile lizard that hunts its prey by day, the water monitor becomes inactive in periods of drought.

Illustrations Steve Roberts/Wildlife Art Agency

THE SUNDARBANS

The Sundarbans region is situated to the north of the Bay of Bengal. A small part lies in northeast India, but the majority belongs to Bangladesh. The Ganges River flows through the region into the Bay. The region is low lying and prone to flooding.

Dhaka

Calcutta

RUSSELL'S VIPER

The venom squeezed from glands on either side of the viper's head swiftly paralyzes its prey.

WHIP SCORPION

Unlike many scorpions, the nocturnal Asian whip scorpion does not have a sting in its tail.

MUGGER CROCODILE

Distinguished by its short snout and powerful jaws, this crocodile eats both large and small mammals.

FLYING FROG

A tree frog that glides rather than flies, it uses its webbed feet like little parachutes.

WOLF SPIDER

The wolf spider does not spin webs to catch its prey; instead it stalks a likely meal, then pounces on it.

HUNTING

Tigers are formidable hunters. Their excellent sight and hearing enable them to locate prey, while their powerful, streamlined bodies allow them to creep silently toward their chosen victim.

Usually solitary hunters, there have been rare occasions when two tigers have been seen cooperating while hunting a large prey animal. They have large appetites and must eat about 4.4 tons (6 tonnes) of meat a year to survive.

At dusk, tigers begin to roam slowly and silently through their territory, pausing from time to time to listen and look for signs of prey. Some tigers seem to follow a regular pattern when searching for food, as though walking a beat. They are not infallible hunters, however, and it is estimated that only one in twenty attempts results in a kill.

Once the tiger has seen its intended prey, it uses the long grasses as cover and creeps as close as it can, approaching from the side or rear of the animal. It must get to within about 30–85 ft (9–26 m), or its final rush will not be successful.

Like the release of a tightly coiled spring, the tiger launches itself with its extremely powerful

ZEFA

Like its larger relatives, a domestic cat (below) *will also crouch and watch its prey.*

Ardea

 **OUT OF ACTION**

Even powerful predators like tigers must avoid injury when killing their prey. Hungry tigers sometimes attack porcupines, whose sharp quills can become embedded in the tiger's limbs, leaving the tiger crippled and unable to hunt.

For the most part, tigers do not seem to be susceptible to diseases. Rabies occurs very occasionally, and trichinosis has been recorded in captive tigers.

PREY

Tigers are at the top of the food chain, preying on almost all mammals that share their habitat. They are capable of killing animals much larger than themselves.

CHITAL

SAMBAR

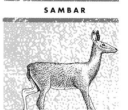

Illustrations Dave Showler/Wildlife Art Agency

Tigers are opportunist hunters and frequently eat fish when in marshy areas.

back legs and pounces on the victim. Often the momentum of the charge knocks the prey to the ground, and the tiger then swipes at it with its huge forepaw. Gripping the prey around the shoulders or back with its forepaws, the tiger bites the animal across the back of the neck, close to the skull. The tiger's hind legs remain firmly on the ground, enabling it to jerk the animal's head back. This severs the spinal cord, crushing the vertebrae and killing the animal.

If the prey is large, or if the tiger has attacked from the front, it will probably go for the animal's throat. The tiger's sharp teeth usually sever vital blood vessels; but even if the jugular is missed, the tiger has enough strength to keep hold of its victim until it dies by suffocation.

A tiger is an immensely powerful hunter, capable

AMAZING FACTS

● The Siberian tiger is capable of eating some 100 lb (45 kg) of meat at one time. This would be like a human eating forty hamburgers in one meal.

● The Siberian tiger sometimes has to walk hundreds of miles in search of food, particularly in the winter months.

● After killing its prey, a tiger always starts feeding from the hindquarters.

THE HUNT IS ON

The tiger has spotted its prey and is crouched, waiting for the right time to pounce. Its eyes fix firmly on the easiest target—a lame buck.

Illustration Barry Croucher/Wildlife Art Agency

GAUR

BEARDED PIG

RHINO

MONKEY

CRAB

WATER BUFFALO

of killing animals over twice its size. When attacking much larger prey, it will often disable it first by lashing out with its powerful forepaws, injuring the prey and bringing it to its knees. At this point, the tiger will pounce on the victim's back and kill it in its preferred way.

Once the prey is dead, the tiger drags or carries it to a secluded place, usually near water and away from scavengers such as vultures and jackals. Feeding begins with the hindquarters of the prey—the tiger strips the skin with its rasping tongue, sharp teeth, and claws.

GETTING CLOSER
The tiger has gotten as close to the prey as it can without being seen.

Anup Shah/Planet Earth Pictures

The tiger (left) drags its meal to a covered place, safe from the eyes of hungry vultures.

An adult Bengal tiger may eat as much as 65 lb (30 kg) of meat in one meal. It will then go to the water to drink. If the prey is large enough, the tiger will cover the remains loosely with leaves and return to feed on it for several nights. During this time, it will remain close to its kill, guarding it from scavengers. Tigers eat every part of their prey, including the lungs, kidneys, and other organs. Unlike most other cats, they will continue to feed on the carcass, even when the meat has started to rot.

A female tiger with young has to kill more often than others to provide enough food for her growing family. She eats only when her cubs have had their fill, keeping a lookout for danger as they feed. It is estimated that she must kill once every five to six days—the equivalent of 60 to 70 animals a year. A lone female without cubs kills about once every eight days, averaging 40 to 50 kills a year.

Cubs learn to hunt by watching their mothers. Perhaps their earliest introduction is when they pounce on the mother's twitching tail. They also learn to stalk and pounce by playing with their mother and their siblings.

CAMOUFLAGE

Against a clear background, the tiger's golden-red-and-black-striped coat stands out clearly. But in the undergrowth of a forest or reed bed, it disappears almost completely.

Tigers are most active at dawn and dusk, when the low-lying sun casts long shadows. The dark stripes on the tiger's sides and back blend in with the shadows of the long grasses through which it creeps, breaking up its distinctive outline. The golden red of its coat helps it disappear into the reddish glow cast by the low sun. At night, the dark colors blend with the forest shadows, making the tiger difficult to see by moonlight.

ZEFA

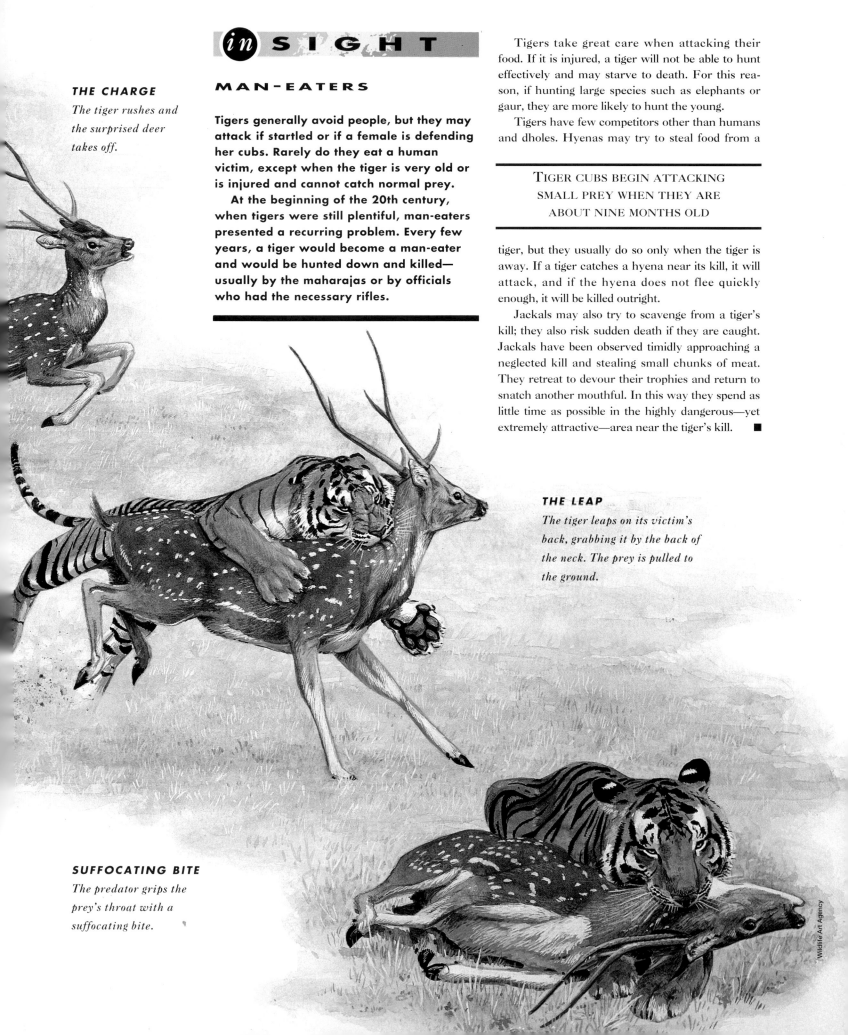

THE CHARGE

The tiger rushes and the surprised deer takes off.

in SIGHT

MAN-EATERS

Tigers generally avoid people, but they may attack if startled or if a female is defending her cubs. Rarely do they eat a human victim, except when the tiger is very old or is injured and cannot catch normal prey.

At the beginning of the 20th century, when tigers were still plentiful, man-eaters presented a recurring problem. Every few years, a tiger would become a man-eater and would be hunted down and killed— usually by the maharajas or by officials who had the necessary rifles.

Tigers take great care when attacking their food. If it is injured, a tiger will not be able to hunt effectively and may starve to death. For this reason, if hunting large species such as elephants or gaur, they are more likely to hunt the young.

Tigers have few competitors other than humans and dholes. Hyenas may try to steal food from a

TIGER CUBS BEGIN ATTACKING
SMALL PREY WHEN THEY ARE
ABOUT NINE MONTHS OLD

tiger, but they usually do so only when the tiger is away. If a tiger catches a hyena near its kill, it will attack, and if the hyena does not flee quickly enough, it will be killed outright.

Jackals may also try to scavenge from a tiger's kill; they also risk sudden death if they are caught. Jackals have been observed timidly approaching a neglected kill and stealing small chunks of meat. They retreat to devour their trophies and return to snatch another mouthful. In this way they spend as little time as possible in the highly dangerous—yet extremely attractive—area near the tiger's kill. ■

THE LEAP

The tiger leaps on its victim's back, grabbing it by the back of the neck. The prey is pulled to the ground.

SUFFOCATING BITE

The predator grips the prey's throat with a suffocating bite.

LIFE CYCLE

Tigers will mate at any time of the year, whenever the female is in season. Female tigers remain in season for only between three and seven days, so they must attract a mate during this time.

A male senses if a female is in season by her scent and will follow her, usually advertising his presence by calling. The female replies and the two tigers eventually meet in the dense undergrowth.

When the tigers meet, they make a facial expression known as the *flehmen* reaction. This is a kind of open-mouthed lip curl, where the tiger wrinkles its nose and sticks out its tongue. The potential mates then indulge in some courtship-playing, which involves mock chases and vicious swipes with the forepaws.

No one has ever seen tigers mating in the wild, but several people have heard them. The female tiger roars and grunts, while the male emits high-pitched squeals and long moans. The actual mating is short, lasting only about 15 seconds, but they may mate as many as 20 times a day, and the courting couple remain together for three to five days.

Once the mating period is over, the tigers separate and the male takes no interest in finding food for the female or helping her raise the cubs.

Gestation lasts for between 95 and 112 days. The tigress continues to hunt almost until the moment of birth, which is generally at night. She finds a quiet spot in dense cover and gives birth very quickly. Then, exhausted, she rests on her side while her cubs begin to suckle.

Tigers can give birth to between one and six cubs, although an average litter is more generally three or four. From this it is usual for one or two cubs to survive to maturity. Tiger cubs measure from 12 to 14 in (30 to 35 cm), with a tail length of about 6 in (15 cm). They are born blind and helpless and are completely dependent on their mother.

Cubs' eyes open after about a week—at about the time when hunger compels the female to leave them to hunt. She leaves at night, hunts quickly, gorges herself, and returns to her young. During the day, the female remains with the cubs. At first, as much as three-quarters of the day is spent suckling the young, but this gradually lessens and they are weaned at five to six months. They cut their milk teeth at the end of the second week; their permanent

AMAZING FACTS

• **The Siberian tiger is unique among tigers in that it develops an insulating layer of fat, sometimes as much as 2 in (5 cm) thick, on its flanks and belly to protect it against the extreme cold.**

• **Sometimes porcupines cause the deaths of tigers. The quills embed themselves in the tiger's feet and legs, rendering the tiger incapable of hunting.**

• **Siberian tigers often become infected with tapeworm, while most Bengal tigers are infested with ticks.**

A family drink. The cubs will not leave the mother's home range until they are about two years old.

THE BIRTH

After a gestation period of about 103 days, the female gives birth to three or four cubs.

MATING

After mating, the male and female remain together for three or four days.

GROWING UP

The cubs remain dependent on their mother for food until the age of eighteen months.

MOVING TIME

Sometimes the mother moves her cubs to a new den. She carries them gently by the scruff of the neck.

M. Donnelly/Wildlife Art Agency

teeth come through after about a year.

After about one month, the mother eats more than she actually needs at a kill. Returning to her cubs, she regurgitates some of the food in a partly digested form for them to eat. By the beginning of the third month, the female brings small chunks of meat back with her for the cubs.

Newborn cubs already have stripes, but the background color of their coats is lighter than that of the adults. Adult coloration comes through at three to six months.

When the cubs are about six months old, the female takes them with her on a hunt. Hiding them in the undergrowth, she makes the kill. Then she calls the cubs to join her and allows them to feast before she feeds herself. By watching her, they learn how to hunt.

LEAVING HOME

The affectionate bond between cubs and mother remains intact and the young stay with her until they are about two years old—longer for Siberian tigers. Male cubs tend to be the first to leave the family unit. When all the cubs have left, the female will come into season again.

When they are first on their own, the young tigers have to find their own hunting grounds. Although other adult tigers will tolerate them passing through their territories, they will attack if they stay too long or if the two come face to face. After a few months, the young tiger will have established its own territory. At four years old it is sufficiently mature to raise cubs of its own, although it is not generally fully grown until it is five.

Most tigers can live up to fifteen years in the wild, although Siberian tigers seem to live longer, sometimes up to twenty years. ∎

FROM BIRTH TO DEATH

BENGAL TIGER

MATING SEASON: USUALLY SPRING
GESTATION: 95–112 DAYS
LITTER SIZE: 2–4 CUBS
WEIGHT AT BIRTH: 33–42 oz (925–1,195 G)

EYES OPEN: 10–14 DAYS
FIRST LEAVE DEN: AT ABOUT 2 MONTHS
INDEPENDENCE: 2 YEARS
SEXUAL MATURITY: 3–4 YEARS
LONGEVITY IN WILD: UP TO 15 YEARS

SIBERIAN TIGER

MATING SEASON: ANY TIME
GESTATION: 95–112 DAYS
LITTER SIZE: UP TO 6 CUBS (AVERAGE 3–4)
WEIGHT AT BIRTH: 28–53 oz (785–1,500 G)

EYES OPEN: 10–15 DAYS
FIRST SOLID FOOD: 14 DAYS
WEANING: 5–6 MONTHS
INDEPENDENCE: 2–3 YEARS
SEXUAL MATURITY: 3–5 YEARS
LONGEVITY: UP TO 20 YEARS

A DYING BREED?

THE DECLINE IN THE NUMBER OF WILD TIGERS THIS CENTURY REPRESENTS A DROP OF OVER **90** PERCENT. UNLESS THE KILLING STOPS NOW, THERE IS NO HOPE FOR THE TIGER

Although they are now protected, tigers are still an endangered species. Of the eight original subspecies, only five are alive today, and all of these are seriously threatened with extinction.

Until the 18th century, tigers were plentiful and were found across Asia. Wherever there was enough vegetation in which to hide and plenty of prey animals, tigers ruled the jungles. Although it is impossible to judge exactly how many tigers there were at this time, their numbers probably exceeded 100,000, with some 40,000 living in India.

Until the middle of the 18th century, tigers were more usually avoided than actively hunted. Human weapons were primitive, and in battles between man and beast, the tiger usually won. But by about 1750, firearms became more efficient, and tiger hunting became a sport for the rich and powerful. At the same time, trade links with Europe improved, and there was a great demand for the luxury woods, such as mahogany, that grew in the Indian forests.

The resulting deforestation destroyed much of the tiger's habitat. Animals that lived in those trees were left without food, and a domino effect was felt throughout the whole food chain. Without food, many herbivores (plant-eaters) either starved to death or moved to other areas. This meant that there were fewer animals on which the tiger could feed, and the tiger was forced into closer contact with humans as it searched for food.

Most Victorians were terrified of tigers. They viewed them as the incarnation of evil, monsters to be destroyed at all costs. But, in true Victorian fashion, they demanded that their death be sporting. Hunts were conducted according to certain rules, with the odds stacked heavily in the hunters' favor.

British army officers and Indian aristocrats viewed tiger-hunting, or shikar as the greatest

E. A. Janes/NHPA

Rearing tigers for the medical trade (above) *is a controversial activity in China.*

Trading in tiger skins is illegal, but the black market will continue where there are consumers (right).

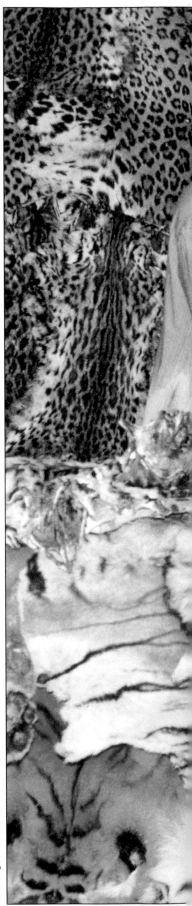

Belinda Wright/Oxford Scientific Films

sport of all. They believed themselves to be incredibly brave, commending each other for their great skill and cool natures. But tigers are naturally fearful of humans, and with increasingly sophisticated weapons, the hunters had, in reality, most of the advantage.

Local people were employed as beaters. They walked through the forests, driving any tigers and other animals into the open and toward the waiting hunters. Sitting high on the backs of fully grown elephants, the hunters shot the tigers as

This map shows the current and former distribution of the tiger.

■ DISTRIBUTION 1993   ▨ DISTRIBUTION 1918

Tigers once roamed throughout Asia. At the beginning of the 20th century, there were some 100,000 tigers living in the wild. Due to human expansion and massive deforestation in the area, there are now less than 9,000 wild tigers. Only 200 Siberian tigers live in the wild.

The Bengal tiger is the most numerous subspecies. It numbers some 3,500 in India, with possibly as many as 1,000 living elsewhere.

The Chinese tiger is on the very brink of extinction. Estimates suggest that just 25 of these animals remain scattered throughout its range. A further 35 Chinese tigers are kept in zoos. The Indochinese tiger numbers about 1,200. These animals are legally protected in Laos, Cambodia, Vietnam, and Thailand, but in Burma they are not protected by law.

The numbers of the Sumatran tiger are feared to be as low as 400. Hunting still goes on, even though they are legally protected. The World Wide Fund for Nature is working with the Indonesian government to try to establish a special preserve for these animals.

It is already too late for the Caspian, Bali, and Javan tigers.

they came into view.

The devastation these hunters caused is truly remarkable. In Nepal, on one shikar (which King George V attended), 39 tigers were killed in just eleven days. The Maharaja of Sarguja killed a staggering 1,157 tigers in his lifetime.

The Indian government at this time also viewed tigers as pests. They were classified as vermin, and anyone who killed one was paid a bounty. The skins of the animals commanded high prices in the West, and hunting was a profitable business.

IN SUMATRA THE TIGER
IS CALLED THE GRANDFATHER
OF THE FOREST

But the decline of the tiger cannot be solely attributed to the hunters. Indeed it was in the hunters' interest to maintain a healthy population to ensure there was always good hunting. Many British officers and local dignitaries maintained the forests, trying to keep the balance of the ecosystem, and they only harvested trees where the forest could regenerate itself.

The biggest danger came from farmers who needed land to grow crops with which to feed their families. They felled huge areas of forest, robbing the tiger of its natural environment. Without its plentiful supply of forest animals, tigers were forced to live closer to humans, so they hunted livestock instead. The farmers retaliated by leaving out poisoned bait for the tiger. Recent figures suggest that local farmers were responsible for about three times as many tiger deaths as the hunters.

in SIGHT

THE TASK AHEAD

All tiger subspecies face extinction. Up to now, governments have had difficulty in cracking down on poachers, smugglers, and middlemen—or they have not wanted to. They must do something now before it is too late. China and Indonesia are beginning to take more and more positive steps to relieve the pressure on the tiger. Education, cooperation, and well-planned conservation must coexist if the tiger is to have a chance of survival. With help and support from the governments concerned, the conservation efforts have a better chance to succeed.

ENDANGERED SPECIES

CHINESE MEDICINE

Throughout the Far East, the tiger is regarded as an animal with magical properties. In Taiwan, tiger wine is made from ground tiger bone. This wine is said to give the drinker special strength. In Malaysia, superstition is such that they believe a single tiger whisker ground up in the animal's flesh is powerful enough to kill an enemy. And in China, some people believe that the clavicle (a small bone found deep in the shoulder muscle) can protect against evil.

TIGER BONES

For centuries the Chinese have believed that tiger products have exceptional medicinal properties. Virtually every part of a tiger's body is used in one remedy or another. Tiger bones are a vital part of many traditional medicines, and even the tiger's penis is highly valued because it is believed to be an aphrodisiac.

Ground tiger bone is believed to cure bad ulcers, rheumatic pain, malaria, and typhoid fever. For rheumatic swellings of joints, the Chinese recommend bathing in tiger-bone broth. Burns and swellings under the toenails can also be treated with powdered tiger bones.

Tiger-bone wine is viewed as a general tonic and energy booster, while traditional beliefs suggest that a piece of tiger bone on the roof will keep the devils away and help cure nightmares.

CONSERVATION MEASURES

If the magnificent tiger is to be saved, the world must act now.

• There are several international conservation groups working to save the tiger (see page 2184), and public support is vital to their work.

• In an attempt to preserve the remaining tigers, the Chinese government has set up a breeding farm that provides animals for both

Tony Stone Worldwide

Poaching, primarily for medicinal purposes, has affected the South China tiger population to such an extent that it is now estimated that less than one hundred individuals remain in the wild.

Tiger bones fetch between $77 and $114 per pound. An average Bengal tiger's skeleton weighs 26.5 lb (12 kg), and even a small tiger may yield 13–15 lb (6–7 kg) of bone. TRAFFIC, an organization set up to monitor the trade of endangered species, estimates that in South Korea alone, some 3,750 lb (1,700 kg) of tiger bones were imported between 1985 and 1990, mainly for the Chinese medicine trade.

THE BAN ON TRADING IN TIGER PRODUCTS HAS BEEN TOTALLY IGNORED BY THIS RETAILER, WHO HOLDS UP A TIGER PENIS IN HIS SHOP.

K. & K. Ammann/Planet Earth Pictures

the medical trade and profit. This is not working to the advantage of either the captive-bred animals or tigers in the wild.

• Taiwan, under the threat of international sanctions, has demanded an all-out effort to crack down on the illegal trade in endangered species. China has followed suit and announced a direct ban on the manufacture, sale, and possession of tiger products. However, enforcement must be strict to impact the market.

TIGERS IN DANGER

THE CHART BELOW SHOWS HOW THE INTERNATIONAL UNION FOR THE CONSERVATION OF NATURE (IUCN), OR THE WORLD CONSERVATION UNION, CLASSIFIES THE STATUS OF THE TIGER. THE YEAR IN BRACKETS IS THE DATE OF CLASSIFICATION:

BENGAL TIGER	ENDANGERED (1993)
INDOCHINESE TIGER	ENDANGERED (1993)
SIBERIAN TIGER	ENDANGERED (1993)
SOUTH CHINA TIGER	ENDANGERED (1993)
SUMATRAN TIGER	ENDANGERED (1993)

ENDANGERED MEANS THAT THE ANIMAL'S SURVIVAL IS UNLIKELY UNLESS STEPS ARE TAKEN TO SAVE IT.

Tom Brakefield/ZEFA

By the beginning of the 20th century, the demand for farmland and towns for people was increasing. Large areas of forest were cleared, without thought for the plants and animals. The high-quality timber was sold, usually to the West.

New species of plants and trees were introduced. These grew quickly, so the cash benefits were realized more easily. However, little thought was given to the effect these plants would have on the local wildlife. Few animals could eat them, which led to a decline in their numbers. With fewer prey animals, the number of tigers fell, too.

In 1972 the Indian government conducted a survey to see how many tigers were remaining. They found that there were just 1,800 tigers left in India.

This story was repeated throughout the tiger's range. The Bali and Caspian tigers were found to be extinct. And the island of Java has been so heavily developed that the Javan tiger subspecies is now extinct.

A survey in Sumatra, however, found that some 600 tigers remained, and in Indochina figures suggest that there were some 2,000 tigers still alive. The Bengal tiger fared slightly better and should not face extinction, provided its habitat is not destroyed further.

Drastic measures were needed to ensure the Bengal cat's survival. The Indian government took the initiative by banning tiger hunting and the export of tiger skins. Local and international conservationists suggested that special areas be set

ENDANGERED SPECIES

2183

ALONGSIDE MAN

When in its natural environment and eating regularly, the tiger usually has a healthy respect for people. Most predators try to avoid costly confrontations, and people are usually associated with danger or, to young tigers, the unknown. But there is no question that tigers are a potential danger to humans. Where respect is mutual, human and animal tragedy is most often avoided.

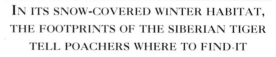

Associated Press/Topham Picture Source

aside as tiger preserves. Their ideas were accepted and Project Tiger was born.

An international appeal for funding was made by His Royal Highness Prince Bernhard of the Netherlands, who was president of the World Wildlife Fund (now called the World Wide Fund for Nature), and more than $1 million was raised.

Indira Gandhi, who was then prime minister, took a personal interest in the project and set up a committee to coordinate action in India. Other countries followed suit and set up tiger preserves in Bangladesh, Nepal, and Bhutan. By 1990 there

Tigers, including this white one, are often trained for nightclub shows. There is much controversy over this practice.

Bottle-feeding a cub is one way of ensuring that a tiger life is safe.

were eighteen specially designated tiger preserves. These include the Sundarbans Reserve, the Royal Chitwan National Park in southern Nepal, and one in the Bhutan Manas forest.

But the problem does not end there. As with all small populations of animals, the number of possible mates is reduced. Within a contained area, a tiger will only come across a certain number of others, and these could well be relatives. Inbreeding can result in a higher incidence of birth defects and can eventually lead to infertility.

Scientists calculate that a group of at least 500

Daniel Heuclin/NHPA

IN ITS SNOW-COVERED WINTER HABITAT, THE FOOTPRINTS OF THE SIBERIAN TIGER TELL POACHERS WHERE TO FIND·IT

individuals is needed to maintain a healthy gene pool and ensure that the species does not suffer genetically. In some preserves, special forest corridors have been established, linking tiger populations. But many preserves are too close to human habitation to allow for this extra band of land, because the local people need it for agriculture.

Another suggestion has been to move individual tigers from one preserve to another, giving them access to tigers that they would not usually meet. This solution does, however, present certain problems: Sedating tigers is always subject to a fair degree of risk.

Captive-breeding programs have been established with the help of many zoos. Records are kept of the parenthood of each tiger to ensure that close relatives are not mated. It has been a great success for the Siberian tiger, and it is now estimated that there are more than twice as many Siberian tigers in captivity as there are in the wild. ■

INTO THE FUTURE

The fate of the tiger is by no means secure. Poaching continues to threaten the animal's survival, but perhaps more seriously, the ongoing destruction of its forest kingdom could well bring about the extinction of these remarkable beasts.

Even the tiger preserves cannot guarantee the tiger's survival. Each area can support only a limited number of cats, which effectively controls their numbers. In the Bardia wildlife preserve in west Nepal, for example, the small amount of land available can support only fifty adult tigers.

Even now natural population controls have been observed. Adult male tigers tend to kill male cubs to reduce future competition for territory. Older males are also being driven off the preserve by young males. The older males then find themselves in areas where there is not enough food to support them, so they attack local farmers' livestock or even the farmers themselves. These animals are then shot or poisoned to reduce the

PREDICTION

WHAT HOPE FOR TIGERS?

With its numbers as low as 25 animals, there is little hope for the South China tiger, and its extinction is imminent. The Siberian and Sumatran tigers could be next to disappear from our world.

risk of attacks on humans.

Destruction of the forest habitat presents further problems for the tiger. Tigers need large areas of good cover for successful hunting. As human populations increase, so does the demand for fertile agricultural land to farm. Land is also needed for houses and towns.

In order for the tiger to survive in the wild, its habitat must also be protected. This means that countries must preserve their forests. But poorer countries, like India, Bangladesh, and Nepal, need more than just international goodwill. They are democracies, and many of the voters do not like seeing the good, fertile land being set aside for what they view as potential man-eaters. Help must be given to these countries if the tiger and its habitat are to survive. ∎

THE TIGER TRUST

The Tiger Trust is an international wildlife foundation dedicated to the conservation and preservation in the wild of all endangered tiger subspecies.

The trust's founder, Michael (Tiger Mike) Day, traveled to Thailand in January 1990 to film the elusive Indochinese tiger. When his favorite, "The Big Boy," was shot by poachers, a crisis was reached and, together with his wife, Sophy, he set up the trust to attract international support for tiger conservation.

In 1992 the Tiger Trust financed and built a natural habitat enclosure for tigers seized in illegal commerce. It is believed to be the largest of its kind in the world.

Education programs, conservation projects, public awareness campaigns, and cooperation with establishing new sanctuaries are some of the ways in which the trust is fighting for tigers.

John Morris/Wildlife Art Agency

VOLES

RELATIONS

Voles and lemmings belong to the suborder Myomorpha, or mouselike rodents. Other members of the suborder include:

RATS & MICE

BLIND MOLE RATS

BAMBOO RATS

ORIENTAL DORMICE

MADAGASCAN RATS

HAMSTERS

GERBILS

Pakka Helo/Bruce Coleman Ltd.

TUNNELS IN THE TURF

VOLES AND LEMMINGS ARE THE HIDDEN MULTITUDE OF THE NORTHERN LANDS, ABUNDANT YET INCONSPICUOUS AS THEY SCURRY AND BURROW THROUGH UNDERGROWTH AND SOIL

The world has more species of rodents than of any other order of mammals, and the mouselike rodents are the most numerous among these. Within this large and complex collection of small mammals, the voles and lemmings form a distinct group—a subfamily divided into three closely related tribes. Between them, the tribes contain 18 genera and a total of 110 species.

ORDER

Rodentia
(rodents)

SUBORDER

Myomorpha
(mouselike rodents)

FAMILY

Muridae

SUBFAMILY

Microtinae
(lemmings and voles)

TRIBES

Lemmini
(lemmings)
Ellobiini
(mole-voles)
Microtini
(voles)

O f all the many groups of rodents, none are so closely associated with the cool, northern climates of Eurasia and North America as the voles and lemmings. Across the temperate grasslands and broad-leaved woods, the cold, dark coniferous forests, and the frigid, open tundra, these are among the most numerous of any mammals. Small and skulking, they are difficult to spot as they forage among ground layers of vegetation or burrow through leaf litter and soil. Yet they exist in such numbers, even in terrain whitened for months by snow, that they play a pivotal role in the ecosystem. Many carnivores depend on them for food, and the breeding success of the hunters is intimately tied to the population rises and falls of their prey.

Voles and lemmings are small, compactly built rodents. At first sight they could be mistaken for mice or rats, but they have more rounded muzzles, smaller eyes and ears, and short tails.

2187

Several million years ago, at least, the lemmings and voles evolved out of the ancestral mouselike stock as a distinct group. They originated in the Eurasian landmass and spread rapidly during the subsequent ice ages when ice fields, building up on the continents, caused a fall in sea level and exposed a land bridge between Siberia and Alaska.

During the heights of the ice ages, voles and lemmings in both Eurasia and North America were able to spread well to the south of their present ranges because conditions there were cooler. After each ice age, when warmer climates returned, the animals retreated north once again.

REMAINS OF COLLARED LEMMINGS, WHICH EXIST TODAY MAINLY IN ARCTIC AND SUBARCTIC HABITATS, HAVE BEEN FOUND IN THE MID-UNITED STATES

Some of the retreating species, however, appear to have been left behind—relict populations that either found the cool conditions they needed up-slope, in mountain ranges, or managed to adapt to the warming climate. This may explain the presence of isolated vole species in the highlands of Mexico.

Today there are some 110 species of voles and lemmings in existence, most of them distributed across the temperate and cold lands of Europe, Asia, and North America, or in upland refuges to the

Wayne Lankinen/Aquila

The American muskrat (above) *has been widely trapped for its pelt.*

2188

The collared lemmings (below) *are tough survivors, venturing as far north as the Arctic ice fields.*

Alan Williams/NHPA

south. On the grasslands and tundra habitats within these zones, they are usually the most abundant mammals. Several general features of the voles and lemmings help account for their success.

SECRET OF THEIR SUCCESS

Voles and lemmings eat and digest a food source on which many other rodents cannot subsist—grass and other coarse herbage—which gives them access to an extremely abundant food supply. They are also adept at either burrowing into the soil or pushing their way through leaf litter and dense ground cover. This provides them with protection from predators and harsh weather, and also brings them in contact with hidden food sources, such as plant roots and seeds.

Adaptations to cool and cold climates enable many voles and lemmings to exploit habitats where there is little competition from other rodents. Unlike many mammals, they do not need to hibernate. Some voles and most lemmings inhabit regions cold enough to have thick snowfall for much of the winter, but because the animals can burrow and tunnel through snow, it actually helps them keep warm by providing a blanket of insulation against the elements. Moreover, their thick fur and compact form help them fight off the chill.

THREE TRIBES

Lemmings and voles together form a subfamily of rodents, itself split into three tribes: lemmings, mole-voles, and voles. The lemmings are the most resistant to cold and tend to have long, dense fur that virtually hides their ears. Collared lemmings

The bank vole makes its home in woodland, scrub, and hedgerows, where food is plentiful.

Abraham Cardwell/Aquila

THE VOLES' & LEMMINGS' FAMILY TREE

and brown lemmings (which include the Norway lemming) are animals of the arctic and subarctic, while the single species of wood lemming inhabits cold coniferous forest. Bog lemmings, which prefer moist habitats, range the farthest south, occurring in isolated sites in the central United States.

The mole-voles (or mole-lemmings), as their name suggests, are specially adapted for underground life. They use their enlarged incisor teeth to dig extensive branching burrows, and their rather cylindrical body shape and velvety fur help them slip through the tunnels. The two species live in fairly dry regions of central Asia.

The vole tribe contains the majority of species, occupying a variety of lowland and upland habitats across North America and Eurasia. Members of this group typically forage among ground vegetation, are about the size of a mouse, and are short-tailed. This description closely fits most of the meadow voles (including the field vole, the meadow vole, the common vole, and the tundra vole), the oriental voles, the steppe lemmings, and the mountain voles.

BREAKING THE MOLD

There are a number of genera or species that in various ways break the mold. The red-backed voles, bank voles, and tree voles, for example, spend much of the time climbing bushes and trees, while the pine voles spend most of their time underground. The water vole is about the size of a rat and finds much of its food in water, while the muskrat, which is nearly twice as large again, has partially webbed hind feet and a long, flattened tail to help it swim. ■

Working out the evolutionary links and relationships between the great assemblage of mammals classed as rodents is a difficult and controversial task. Not all zoologists would accept the family tree outlined here, but it reflects the views most widely held. It shows the lemmings and voles arising from the general group of mouselike rodents. The lemmings and voles further subdivide into three tribes: the lemmings, the mole-voles, and the voles.

FIELD VOLE
Microtus agrestis
(m i e - C R O A T - u s
a h - G R E S T - i s)

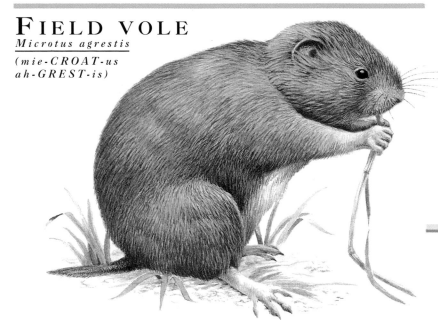

Like most members of the Microtini tribe, field voles possess blunt snouts, fairly small ears and eyes, and short tails in relation to body length. They are also stoutly built. Microtini is the largest of the three tribes, with 13 genera and a total of 99 species.

SQUIRREL-LIKE RODENTS

CAVYLIKE RODENTS

Norway Lemming

Lemmus lemmus (LEM-us LEM-us)

The tribe Lemmini consists of four genera: the brown lemmings, which includes the Norway lemming; the collared lemming; the wood lemming, and the bog lemming. The nine species, which live mainly in cold regions, have stout, compact bodies, long fur, and short tails.

Mole-vole

Ellobius (eh-LOBE-ee-us)

Known alternatively as mole-lemmings, there are two species in the tribe Ellobiini: the northern mole-vole, E. talpinus, and the southern mole-vole, E. fuscocapillus. They occupy grassland and semidesert areas, and their velvety fur, tiny ears, small eyes, and jutting incisor teeth are adaptations for lives spent underground.

Mouselike Rodents

All Rodents

ANATOMY:
THE LEMMING

Most species have a head-and-body length of 4–4.5 in (10–11 cm), with a tail around 1.2–1.6 in (3–4 cm) long. These are typified by the Norway lemming (far left) and bank vole (left). Largest of the subfamily is the muskrat, which grows to the size of a small rabbit.

THE EARS

are barely visible among the thick fur, yet, are extremely sensitive to sound.

BODY SHAPE

is crucial to a lemming's survival. The stocky, compact, blunt-headed build of the Norway lemming minimizes the animal's surface area, helping it retain body heat in the cold tundra climate.

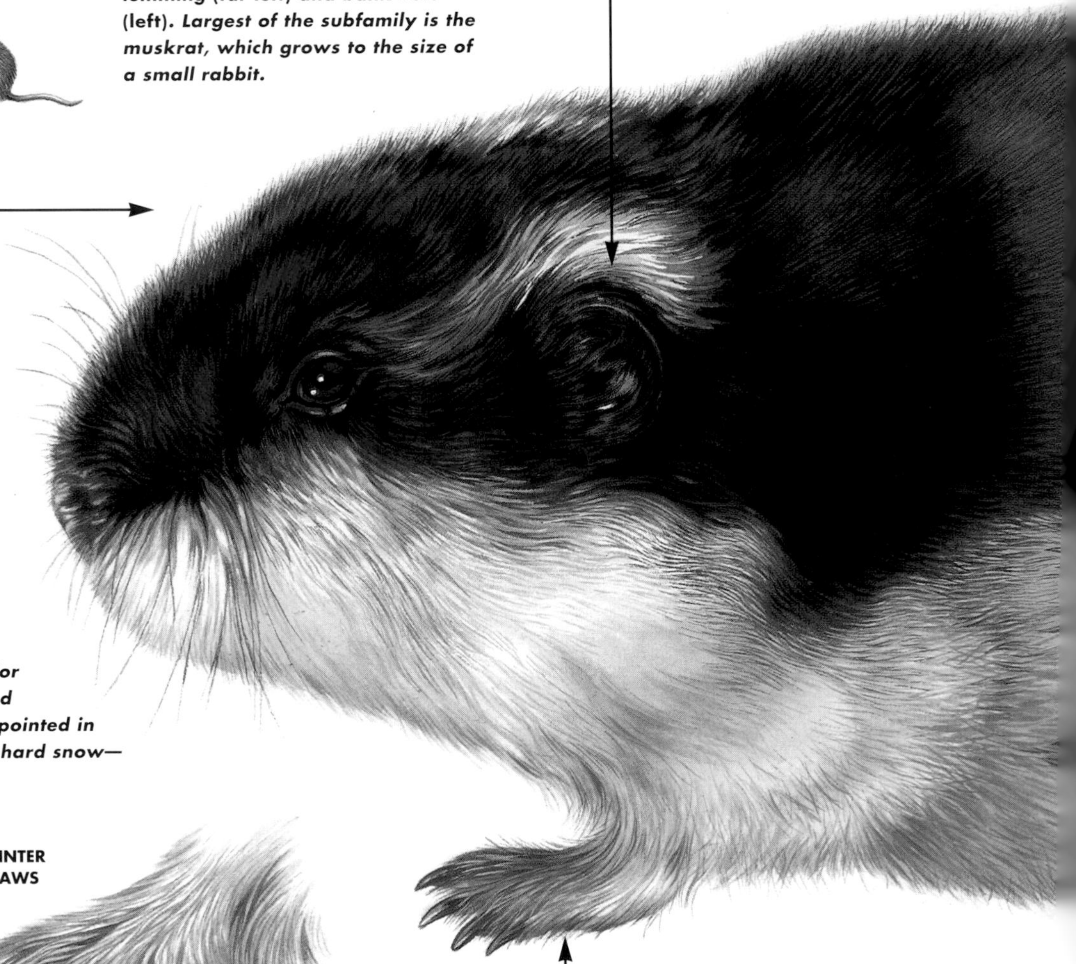

Collared lemmings have specialized forefeet for burrowing in snow. The claws on the third and fourth toes are enlarged and become double-pointed in winter as an adaptation to breaking through hard snow—a feature unique among rodents.

NORMAL CLAWS

WINTER CLAWS

THE FOREFEET

are used for burrowing through snow. The claw on the first digit is broad and flattened to aid digging.

SKELETON

The skeleton of the Norway lemming reveals the animal's compact, stocky body shape, along with the shortness of the limb bones. Short legs make crawling through tight burrows easier, as well as further reducing the animal's surface area to improve heat retention.

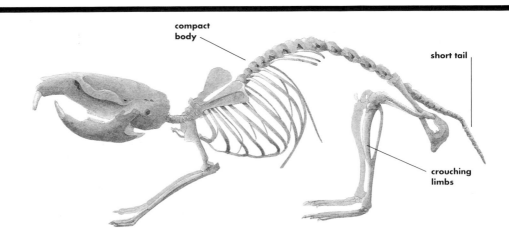

compact body

short tail

crouching limbs

X-ray illustrations Elisabeth Smith

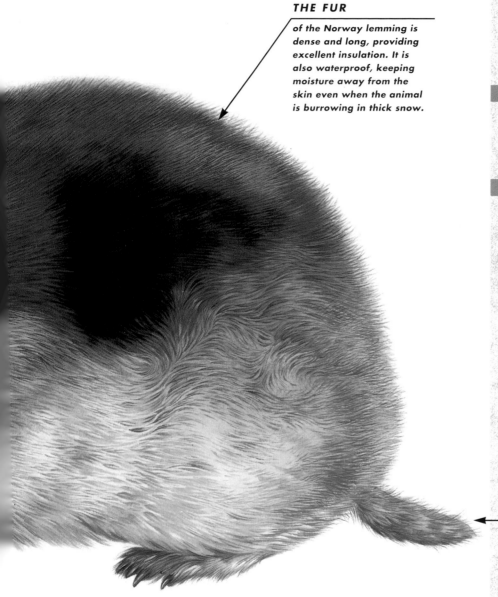

THE FUR

of the Norway lemming is dense and long, providing excellent insulation. It is also waterproof, keeping moisture away from the skin even when the animal is burrowing in thick snow.

F ACT F ILE:

THE NORWAY LEMMING

CLASSIFICATION

GENUS: *LEMMUS*

SPECIES: *LEMMUS*

SIZE

HEAD–BODY LENGTH: 5–6 IN (130–150 MM)

TAIL LENGTH: 0.5–0.8 IN (15-20 MM)

WEIGHT: 2–4 OZ (50–115 G)

WEIGHT AT BIRTH: 0.1–0.12 OZ (3-3.5 G)

COLORATION

VARIEGATED BLACK, YELLOWISH BROWN, AND BUFF ON THE UPPER BODY, MUCH PALER (OFTEN WHITE) ON THE UNDERSIDE

FEATURES

STOCKY, COMPACT SHAPE

BROAD, ROUNDED HEAD

EARS ALMOST HIDDEN BY FUR

MEDIUM-LENGTH WHISKERS

VERY SHORT TAIL

SHORT LEGS

THE TAIL

is short and typical of burrowing animals. Like the ears and limbs, its small size helps reduce heat loss in cold climates.

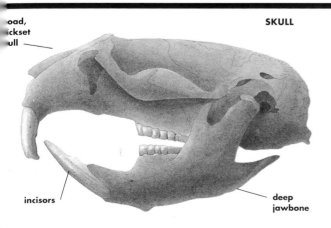

broad, thickset skull

incisors

SKULL

deep jawbone

The Norway lemming has a short, thickset skull. The strong jawbones have large muscles to help the animal process tough plant matter.

TEETH
Lemmings and voles have twelve molar teeth, with flattened crowns for grinding food. The four incisors are used for cutting. Some voles have continuously growing molars that counteract the wear induced by eating coarse grasses.

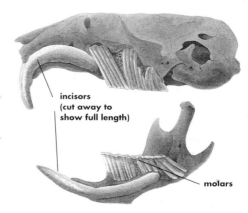

incisors (cut away to show full length)

molars

CYCLES OF LIFE

DAY AND NIGHT, THE PASSAGE OF THE SEASONS, AND THE SWINGS BETWEEN GOOD YEARS AND BAD: ALL AFFECT THE BEHAVIOR OF VOLES AND LEMMINGS

I n virtually all aspects of their existence, voles and lemmings exhibit regular patterns of behavior. There is the daily cycle of activity through night and day. Then there is a seasonal change in habits, accentuated in northerly lands. Lastly, there is a periodic cycle of a few years' duration: a regular rise and fall in the populations of many voles and lemmings that affects their behavior—often dramatically.

Voles and lemmings spend much of their time foraging energetically for food. Some are active by day, others emerge at night. Many can be active at any time but are most busy around dawn or dusk, when the long shadows provide security.

Michael Leach/NHPA

THE SAGEBRUSH VOLE IS MOST ACTIVE FOR TWO TO FOUR HOURS AT DAWN AND FOUR TO SIX HOURS AROUND SUNSET

Voles tend to use established routes through dense vegetation—these show up as narrow trails of trampled and cut leaves or as tunnels through tall grasses. The prairie vole also scatters dirt over its runways to lay trails up to 2 in (5 cm) wide. Runways may be maintained even in the winter snows—the Punjab vole is one of many species that dig tunnels through snow, lining them with soil and vegetation.

Radiating patterns of runways lead to burrow entrances. Most voles and lemmings burrow at least to some extent, although the depth and extent of diggings vary considerably according to the species. Using their feet and teeth to dig through soil and cut roots, they may create burrows with several galleries and chambers for shelter, food storage, and breeding. A single collared lemming may maintain up to fifty burrows in its territory for ready retreat when threatened.

The water vole (above) *tunnels into riverbanks and fields. It has few special adaptations to life in the water, but it can nevertheless swim very well—even along the riverbed.*

Muskrats (right) *are natural swimmers but awkward on land. Supreme architects, they build extensive burrow systems with underwater entrances and ventilation shafts.*

WINTER MOLT

Tom McHugh/Oxford Scientific Films

The collared lemmings of the arctic tundra undergo a remarkable change each year. Colored in shades of buff, brown, and gray in summer, they molt in autumn and grow a pelt of pure white fur. Several other animals of the cold lands turn white in winter, too, among them the arctic fox, the arctic hare, the ermine, and the ptarmigan. But the collared lemmings are the only rodents that do so. The white fur provides the lemmings with excellent camouflage in an open landscape coated with snow during the winter.

Voles and lemmings build sleeping nests at any time of the year and, in the breeding season, for rearing young. Placed in a burrow or rock crevice or among foliage, they are generally rounded structures of shredded herbage, lichen, and twigs. Many species change their nesting habits depending on the season. Brown lemmings and the heather vole nest in shallow burrows in summer but relocate to the surface in winter. Hidden under an insulating blanket of snow, they can then place their nests in safety among rocks or at the bases of shrubs.

Wary when foraging and concealed when not, voles and lemmings are by and large secretive animals. But another remarkable side to their behavior periodically comes to light. In some voles and most lemmings, every few years the population moves into an exceptionally rapid breeding phase and numbers quickly build up to pressure point. Forced by dwindling food and space, large numbers of the animals migrate to find unoccupied land. During this behavior they are much more visible than normal and put themselves at high risk of attack from predators. ∎

Tom Ulrich/Oxford Scientific Films

HABITATS

Though the most familiar species of voles and lemmings are associated with the cooler environments of North America and Eurasia, the group as a whole has adapted to most habitat types available in these continents. Among the meadow voles alone, there is a wide range of habitat preferences. The tundra vole is at home on the bleak, open tundra, and the taiga vole lives in the northern conifer forests. The prairie vole inhabits dry grasslands, while the American water vole is fond of upland meadows close to streams. The snow vole is associated with rocky highlands, but Townsend's vole occupies coastal salt marshes.

COLLARED LEMMINGS ARE KNOWN TO
CROSS COASTAL PACK ICE TO REACH
OUTLYING ISLANDS

There are mountain voles in the ranges of central Asia, well above the tree line. One of these has a curious flattened skull, probably an adaptation to sheltering under rocks. The heather vole prefers scrubby areas and open glades in conifer forests, while the sagebrush vole inhabits semiarid habitats with a covering of brush and bunchgrasses. The mole-voles also live in dry grasslands and semi-deserts, but the bog lemmings are animals of cold, moist habitats such as bogs and springs.

Many lemmings and voles are fairly specialized in their habitat choice, so that though they appear

Bomford & Borkowski/Ardea

KEY FACTS

● A valley in northwestern Nevada was overrun with voles in 1907–1908. At that time the density of montane voles in the area reportedly reached 8,000–12,000 per acre (20,000–30,000 per hectare).

● Though the common vole does not occur in mainland Britain, races of this species occur in the Orkney Islands north of Scotland, as well as on Guernsey in the Channel Islands. All are larger than their European counterparts.

● Several vole species are adapted for life in the mountains, among them the Kashmir vole, the Punjab vole, and the snow vole, which lives in Europe.

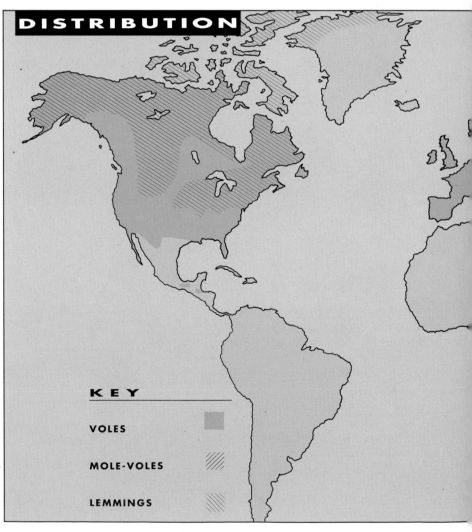

DISTRIBUTION

KEY

VOLES

MOLE-VOLES

LEMMINGS

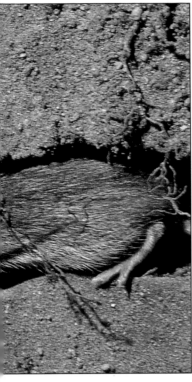

The American pine vole (left) *spends most of its life underground, although it rarely burrows deeper than the loose soil and decomposing mulch near the surface.*

Like many voles, the bank vole (right) *digs special sleeping chambers, lining them with dried grasses for warmth and comfort.*

Rodger Jackman/Oxford Scientific Films

Voles and lemmings are found in North America, Europe, and Asia, from the high Arctic to subtropical zones. Of the three tribes, the voles have the widest distribution, both east to west and north to south. The lemmings are also widely distributed, but they are more closely linked to the northern lands. The mole-voles, by contrast, live in semideserts and steppes from Ukraine and Turkey east across central Asia to Mongolia.

to have overlapping ranges, they avoid competition by concentrating in different types of terrain. The Arctic and Siberian lemmings, for example, both share large tracts of the Eurasian tundra, but the former prefers drier, upland tundra, while the latter is more predominant in damp lowland sites where grasses and sedges can grow. But some voles are flexible in their habitat choices. The field vole is associated with open, grassy places, but these may

---

THE MOUNTAIN VOLES OF CENTRAL ASIA HAVE BEEN FOUND AT ALTITUDES AS GREAT AS 18,800 FT (5,700 M)

---

be in ungrazed meadows, the edges of cultivated fields, the shoulders of roads, open woodland such as birch forest or conifer clearings, moorland, or seaside dunes. The bank vole likes a more closely wooded habitat with thick undergrowth, but is also common in hedgerows and scrubland.

BANK VOLES IN THE BRANCHES

Most of the species mentioned so far are essentially ground-dwellers that spend their lives among grass, undergrowth, rocks, and leaf litter or burrow into the soil. Not all voles, however, are confined to the ground. The bank vole and its close relative the northern red-backed vole are both able climbers and regularly ascend into bushes and low trees to feed. The red-tree vole, which lives in the humid temperate forests on the western coast of the United States, is even more at home above the ground. Though the males live in burrows and climb into trees mainly to feed and mate, the females stay in the branches. They are not particularly agile, since their movements are deliberate and they require a firm grip on the next support before releasing a foothold, yet they may forage high in the tree canopy. Females build their nests of twigs and pine needles up to 50 ft (15 m) above the ground on the forks of branches or on the abandoned nests of birds or squirrels.

TAILS OF THE RIVERBANK

A few voles spend a good deal of their time in rivers and ponds. Most voles can swim a little when the need arises, but the European water vole is particularly aquatic. Though it has no obvious adaptations for swimming, it freely enters water and can dive easily to the bed of slow-flowing streams, canals, and pools. In many parts of its range it prefers to live at the waterside and excavates its burrows in riverbanks. Should danger threaten, the water vole slips quickly into the water and into the entrance tunnel of its burrow, which is often located below the waterline—beyond the reach of terrestrial predators.

The muskrat, the most atypical of all the voles, is yet more aquatic in habits. A large rodent, it swims and dives well, using its partly webbed hind feet as

paddles and its long, flattened tail as a rudder. Muskrats make their homes in marshes, swamps, ponds, lakes, and rivers, either digging deep burrows in banks using their teeth and claws, or building large mounds of stems, reeds, and mud reminiscent of beavers' lodges. Nest chambers inside the burrows and mounds remain dry, but the entrances to both are under water, positioned below the maximum depth to which the water freezes in winter. Muskrats will often clear channels through thickly growing water plants to ensure easy access to and from their nests. ∎

FOCUS ON

THE SCANDINAVIAN TUNDRA

The tundra, home of the Norway lemming, is a harsh but beautiful environment of open, rolling high ground, where trees are merely knee-high shrubs. Between the rocky outcrops, the soil is scattered with low plants, such as dwarf willow, avens, heather, mosses, and lichens. In low ground, the terrain is often boggy, with a thicker growth of grasses and sedge. In the dark winter, temperatures plummet and blizzards howl; food is scarce and few animals are active. In summer, the climate warms enough for plants to bloom. Insects abound, and birds visit to breed. The topsoil thaws out, allowing seedlings to take root and animals to burrow.

The changing seasons force the Norway lemming to move home twice a year. In summer, it digs short, shallow burrows on the open slopes, lining its sleeping and breeding burrows with grass and fur. Winter drives it back to more sheltered sites, often into the grassy lower slopes where snow lies thick. The lemming digs a nest cavity into the drifts, filling it with a cozy, hollow ball of dry grass, mosses, and lichen. The lemming forages through the winter, tunneling through the snow to reach food. With the arrival of the spring thaw, the lemming loses its protective blanket, and its low-lying nesting area soon becomes boggy. It is then time to move back onto drier ground.

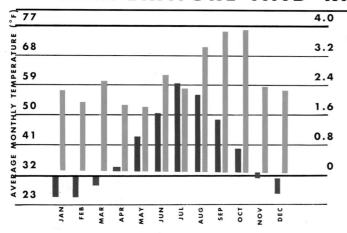

TEMPERATURE AND RAINFALL

■ TEMPERATURE
▨ RAINFALL

Lying so far north, the Scandinavian tundra has weak sunshine even in summer. For part of the winter, the sun never appears, and the climate is bitterly cold. The snow lies for many months, but overall rainfall is low.

NEIGHBORS

Not all tundra animals hibernate or move south in winter. Many simply change their pelt or plumage for a camouflaging white coat, to help them go about their day hidden from predators.

ARCTIC HARE

The arctic hare grows a white winter coat to help conceal it while foraging in the snowy landscape.

WOLVERINE

The wolverine is a powerful hunter, able to chase and bring down reindeer in the thick tundra snow.

Illustrations Jo Cowne/Wildlife Art Agency

The Scandinavian tundra extends across the northern reaches of Scandinavia, taking in parts of Norway, Sweden, and Finland, as well as the Kola Peninsula of Russia. The tundra is a harsh, sparsely populated land—the only sector of mainland Europe that lies within the arctic circle.

DISTRIBUTION OF NORWAY LEMMING

NORWAY

FINLAND

SWEDEN

RUSSIA

E N E M I E S

EXTREMELY DANGEROUS

Lemmings are particularly vulnerable to the snowy owl in summer. The bird swoops to snatch them as they scurry along their runways.

EXTREMELY DANGEROUS

The arctic fox is one of many tundra animals that prey on the Norway lemming. In winter, it often digs deep into snow to try to catch them.

STOAT	GYRFALCON	WOLF	PTARMIGAN	SNOW BUNTING

The ermine or stoat is a deadly predator, slender enough to pursue lemmings into their burrows.

The gyrfalcon is a powerful bird of prey that scours the tundra for victims—mainly rodents and nesting birds.

Its howl was once a familiar sound on the tundra, but today the wolf has been hunted into rarity.

The ptarmigan's plumage is white in winter; in summer its gray feathers match the thawed ground.

Snow buntings come to the tundra to nest when the summer warmth makes food more plentiful.

FOOD AND FEEDING

Voles and lemmings feed largely on the green parts of low-growing herbaceous plants—on grass blades, leaves, and shoots—though many also eat seeds, berries, nuts, lichens, twigs, and bark. As well as foraging on the surface, most also dig to gnaw roots and bulbs. Several species also eat animal food from time to time, among them the bog lemmings, which sometimes eat slugs and snails, and the water vole, which sometimes takes aquatic invertebrates. Altogether, a vole or lemming feeds for at least several hours per day and may consume its own body weight in food in a 24-hour period.

As the months pass and different food sources abound or dwindle, voles and lemmings often need to adapt their feeding habits. For the surface-feeders, this may mean turning from green herbage in summer to less nutritious foods still available in winter. The field vole often chews bark in winter, for example, while the Norway lemming relies

Anthony & Elizabeth Bomford/Ardea

THE WATER VOLE NOT ONLY FINDS ROOTS TO EAT IN ITS OWN BURROWS, BUT IT ALSO BREAKS INTO THE TUNNEL SYSTEMS OF MOLES—TO LOCATE FOOD THE EASY WAY

The bank vole (above) *often stockpiles hazelnuts or berries for the winter, especially if there is a bumper crop. It may bury them in the soil or store them in tree holes and abandoned birds' nests.*

largely on mosses. But winter snows can also open up new feeding possibilities. The sagebrush vole can burrow up through deep snow to reach shrubs that are too high to reach in summer.

Those voles that can climb shrubs and trees typically enjoy a wider variety of foods. The bank vole, for instance, eats as much seed and fruit from trees as it does herbage. It also consumes roots and fungi and cuts neat holes in hazelnuts to extract the kernels. But the specialist red tree vole is one climber that has a curiously limited diet. It survives largely on pine needles, which are highly abundant in its forest home but very difficult to digest.

Other voles with atypical habits similarly have atypical feeding behaviors. For those that spend most of their time burrowing, food is almost wholly the underground parts of plants: roots, bulbs, and tubers. Pine voles tunnel down to gnaw into, and up through, the stems of herbaceous plants, including cultivated crops.

MOLE-VOLES

obtain their food underground as they tunnel. As well as using their incisors to gnaw through roots, they devour flower bulbs and tubers.

Illustrations Kim Thompson

(in)SIGHT

WINTER STORES

Many species of voles and lemmings store some of the excess food they gather in summer and autumn. These hidden caches can then be drawn upon during the winter months, when nutritious food is generally less plentiful and weather conditions can make foraging difficult. Mountain voles typically cut grass stems and leaves and let them dry in the sunshine, then stuff these caches of "hay" into rock crevices. The bank vole often hides nuts, berries, and seeds in small holes it digs in the soil and then fills the holes again with dirt.

Vole species that dig complex burrows, with nesting and resting chambers, often also have special food storage chambers for their winter supplies. The prairie vole's food chamber may be nearly 3 ft (1 m) in length. Laboratory studies show that this food-caching behavior is triggered instinctively when daylight length decreases past a certain level.

THE WATER VOLE

eats grasses and waterside plants. It chews through the bases of reed stems to topple the plants, and holds the plant portions in its forepaws to eat.

The muskrat finds its food both in and out of the water. Its main sources are waterside plants such as sedges, horsetails, and rushes. It also eats aquatic plants, such as water lilies and pondweed, and forages for berries, twigs, and cultivated crops on dry land. It often eats just a small part of the plants it cuts—usually the bases of sedge stems, for example, which are richest in carbohydrates and protein. The muskrat also eats aquatic prey such as shellfish, crayfish, frogs, and even fish. In marshy areas, it prefers to carry its food to a special platform of vegetation and mud similar to, but smaller than, its nest mound. Here it goes ahead and eats, safe from mink or foxes. ■

TERRITORIES

The social lives of voles and lemmings have been the subject of much study in recent years, revealing behavior patterns that are both complex and variable. Factors such as gender, age, habitat, diet, population density, and the changing seasons all play their part.

CALLING CARDS

Since they spend most of the time hidden from view, voles and lemmings communicate with one another largely by sound and scent. Each species has its own particular calls, and, by leaving scent marks in its habitat, a rodent can leave messages behind for others of its kind, indicating that it is at large. Feces, droplets of urine, or secretions from scent glands can all be used. The water vole rubs its hind feet over special glands on its flanks and then scrapes the scent onto a spot on the ground.

When two members of the same species physically encounter each other, the outcome is often antagonistic. One will usually try to assert dominance over the other, and fighting is not uncommon, especially between members of the same sex. The

Female water voles are not normally territorial. In the breeding season, however, they secure a stretch of riverbank (below) *and defend it aggressively.*

John Morris/Wildlife Art Agency

Mike Lane/Aquila

WHEN UNDER PRESSURE

from a local population boom or a scarcity of food, lemmings take it out on each other. Fights may be brief or bloody, but the net result is usually a mass migration of a large number of individuals to new pastures.

sense of home—that space a lemming or vole will try to defend against intruders—varies greatly. Collared lemmings tend to concentrate on defending their nesting burrows alone, while a female bank vole will actively defend her home range around the nest as well. By making the home range a strict territory, the bank vole tries to secure an exclusive supply of seeds, berries, and herbage—foods that are more patchily distributed than grass.

Sex and age can create marked differences in territoriality. In the field vole, adult males defend large exclusive territories; mature females have fixed home ranges but these are small and freely overlap with those of other females; and subadults are nomadic. In some voles, among them the taiga vole and the prairie vole, territoriality breaks down outside the breeding season to such an extent that groups of the rodents share communal burrows and even huddle together for warmth while nesting.

Even so, the group remains incohesive and bickering is frequent. Aggression at this time can cause young males in particular to disperse from the established area to new grounds.

POPULATION DENSITIES

The size of the typical home range once again varies considerably from species to species—from just a few square yards around the burrow in the case of some lemmings to a maximum of seven acres (2.75 ha) recorded for the taiga vole in northern Canada.

> COLLARED LEMMINGS LEAVE AN AREA ONLY WHEN FORCED TO DO SO BY A LACK OF FOOD

In many voles the average is less than one acre (0.4 ha), resulting in a typical population density in favorable habitats of one or two individuals per acre (less than half a hectare). In some years when the population rapidly grows, densities quickly rise, in some cases to several hundred per acre (less than half a hectare). During these peak periods of intense overcrowding, behavior can change radically, with territories becoming a fraction of their normal size, a rash of aggressive behavior, and the dramatic exodus of large numbers of the animals. ■

GOOD NEIGHBORS

The common vole often lives in clusters, with several animals digging their extensive burrows close together or even sharing a burrow. There is little evidence, however, of social organization among the neighboring voles.

LIFE CYCLE

Breeding in voles and lemmings proceeds at a hectic pace. In general, the animals develop fast, mature early, and bear large numbers of young in rapid succession. But, typically, voles and lemmings exhibit considerable variation from species to species and from region to region.

Most species are physically capable of breeding in both summer and winter, and lemmings, despite the harshness of their winter environment, regularly do so. Voles living in temperate climes, however, tend to produce most of their young over the spring and summer, when food is most plentiful. Bank and field voles start breeding in earnest in April and the season draws to a close around October. In voles of Mediterranean regions, breeding tends to fall either side of the dry summer, concentrated in the wetter periods of spring and autumn.

NORWAY

lemmings can breed through the winter, mating in their burrows under the deep snow.

THE YOUNG

start to feed for themselves in the third week. Soon they themselves will be ready for breeding.

A FEMALE LEMMING FORMS A CLOSE BOND WITH HER YOUNG. SHE GROOMS THEM REGULARLY, AND THEIR FUR ACQUIRES A LUSTROUS, SILKY SHEEN

Females carry the developing young for up to four weeks before giving birth, though in some species gestation can be as short as sixteen days. For their forthcoming offspring, females prepare cozy nests composed of dry grass or other plant material and more often than not hidden in a subterranean chamber. In all but a few species of voles, the females make their preparations alone. The males have no bond with their mating partners and search for successive mates throughout the season; their instinct is to sire as many young as possible. In some cases, notably in the collared lemming, male newcomers approaching a nesting female have been known to kill her existing young before trying to mate with her.

Each mature female gives birth on average to two to four litters in a normal breeding season, and in exceptional years as many as eight. For the mole-voles, six or seven litters per year is the norm. Cases of females mating within a few hours of giving birth are not uncommon.

A female collared lemming nurses her offspring. She gives birth to her first litter in early summer and will breed again before autumn. Typically there are three or four young in each litter.

GROWING UP

The life of a young Norway lemming

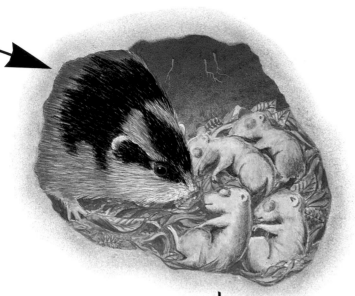

AS THE YOUNG

grow and their eyes open, the female guards them closely. She rarely leaves them, except to retrieve any that have strayed from the nest chamber.

THE FEMALE

typically gives birth to 1–13 tiny, naked young, which she suckles for about two weeks in her underground burrow.

FROM BIRTH TO DEATH

NORWAY LEMMING	WATER VOLE
GESTATION: 16–23 DAYS	**GESTATION:** 20–22 DAYS
LITTER SIZE: 1–13	**LITTER SIZE:** 2–8
BREEDING: YEAR-ROUND IF CONDITIONS ARE FAVORABLE	**BREEDING:** MARCH TO OCTOBER
NO. OF LITTERS: 1–8 PER YEAR	**NO. OF LITTERS:** 1–4 PER YEAR
WEIGHT AT BIRTH: 0.1 oz (3.3 G)	**WEIGHT AT BIRTH:** 0.2 oz (5 G)
EYES OPEN: 11 DAYS	**EYES OPEN:** 8 DAYS
WEANING: 14–16 DAYS	**WEANING:** 14 DAYS
SEXUAL MATURITY: 2–5 WEEKS	**SEXUAL MATURITY:** 8–9 WEEKS
LONGEVITY: 1–2 YEARS	**LONGEVITY:** 5 MONTHS ON AVERAGE

As few as one or two, or as many as 12 or 13, young are born at a time. Tiny, blind and capable only of staggering movements, the newborn huddle together in the shelter of the nest, moving purposely only when searching for a place to cling to the lactating female. But they develop fast. After several days their fur starts to appear, and a few days later their eyes open. As early as two weeks, in some cases, they begin to feed for themselves, and soon they make the first tentative steps into the open.

By this time female young may already be capable of breeding (some actually go into heat while still being suckled); males tend to take just two or three weeks longer to reach sexual maturity. This means that young born early in a breeding season can raise their own young before the season is out.

TRIALS OF LIFE

Voles and lemmings live only one to two years—and the population turnover is high. In a stable breeding population, mortality may be as high as 30 percent of the animals per month. Being small and numerous, voles and lemmings are hunted high and low—by cats, foxes, weasels, owls, falcons, and snakes. Varying food supplies, cold weather, and disease also take their toll. ∎

Illustrations Douglas Ingram

in SIGHT

PRAIRIE PARENTS

The prairie vole, which inhabits the dry grasslands of central North America, is one of the few voles in which males and females form pair bonds. After mating with one female, the males of most other species try to find other mating partners, but prairie voles are monogamous. A mated pair shares the same burrow, and the male cooperates in parental care by grooming the young and retrieving them when they stray too far from the nest, and by keeping the burrow and surface runways clear of debris. In other species, the female alone carries out all the responsibilities of parenthood.

MIGRATION

Voles and lemmings are prolific breeders, in favorable conditions. But there are many factors that usually keep numbers in check in the wild, such as food scarcity, predation, and the spread of diseases. All are more influential when rodent numbers are high, causing population growth to tail off, then reverse. Many voles and lemmings also seem to have a built-in check on their numbers: Excessive crowding affects their reproductive behavior and suppresses their birthrate.

For some voles, there are seasonal fluctuations in population yet no pattern of change from year to year. For others there are peaks and valleys in the population every few years. In peak years, numbers can soar to extraordinary levels before declining. In some meadow voles, the extreme densities result in far-reaching ecological impacts. Pastures may be grazed almost bare, soils riddled by burrows, crops spoiled, and young trees stripped of their bark. Vole predators, meanwhile, enjoy a feeding bonanza.

At the height of a population cycle, it is common for several animals to leave crowded zones for new areas. In steppe lemmings, collared lemmings, and most famously in Norway lemmings, these dispersals are better described as mass migrations.

DESTINATION UNKNOWN

The periodic migrations of the Norway lemming are known as one of nature's strangest phenomena. Scandinavians invented legend—spontaneous generation in rain clouds—to account for the sudden plagues of lemmings around their settlements. They blamed the rodents for devastating crops and fouling water and air with their dying bodies as they marched relentlessly across the land, hell-bent on leaping in mass suicide into the sea.

A snowy owl feeds its nestlings on the flesh of a lemming (above).

The truth behind the lore is no less remarkable. Norway lemmings can breed all year, especially if the winter is mild, and in good years they tend to have larger and more frequent litters. Young animals even become sexually mature quicker in these phases. As a result, every two to five years, numbers reach epidemic proportions, with densities leaping to more than 120 animals per acre (300 per hectare).

At the peak, aggression rises and hordes of lemmings move out. Most of the wanderers are youngsters probably ousted by older, settled individuals. From the tundra, they trek down into birch forests and conifer woods. They scatter haphazardly, but obstacles force them to converge. As their paths meet, the jostling often brings on a blind panic that drives the animals on with renewed momentum—some to a new home, others to oblivion in the cold waters of a river or the jaws of a predator.

The migrants suffer very high mortality, from drowning, exhaustion, predation, and other hazards of the passage. But the notion of mass suicide is misplaced. Migration takes place as a desperate response to overcrowding. Its object is survival, and many of the migrants do succeed in finding and colonizing new habitats, at least temporarily. ∎

MASS PANIC

When living conditions become so crowded that the lemmings find life intolerable, they leave the area for new pastures. Panicking to get away, they set out in vast unstoppable numbers.

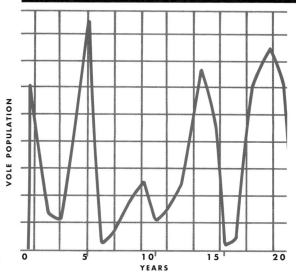

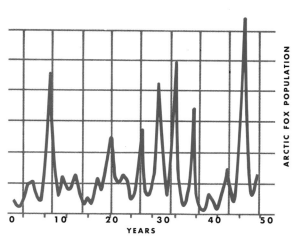

MIGRATING

Marching over fields and into towns, the lemmings even swim rivers. When they run out of land and reach the sea, they blindly try to swim that, too. They struggle bravely against the tides, but death is inevitable.

After a dip in populations, voles and lemmings enter a phase of low mortality and rapid reproduction. But overcrowding sets in, and food becomes short. Breeding is inhibited and mortality rises fast from starvation, attack, and the hazards of dispersal. Numbers crash, and it is a while before normal breeding conditions return.

The populations of some predators are closely geared to those of voles and lemmings: They breed more successfully when prey is abundant. Hence vole or lemming "years" are usually good years for local owls, weasels, and arctic foxes. The charts above show how the multiyear population cycles of predator and prey are related.

WHEN HOME SHRINKS

VOLES AND LEMMINGS MAY BE RENOWNED FOR THEIR PERIODIC POPULATION SURGES AND GENERAL ABUNDANCE, BUT FOR SOME SPECIES AND RACES THE FUTURE IS BY NO MEANS CERTAIN

Voles and lemmings are not noted for their susceptibility to the pressures brought to bear by humans on the survival of so many other mammal species. Indeed, they are better known for their abundance in the countryside and the "plagues" of them that sometimes occur. During peak years, species in temperate regions can be troublesome to farmers and to keepers of orchards and vineyards by causing extensive damage to pastures, crops, and seedlings. And by stripping bark from the bases of the trunks, these rodents can even cause the death of established trees.

Despite these problems, few voles and lemmings suffer the direct persecution meted out to rodents, such as rats or house mice, that conflict more heavily with people. Except for the muskrat, which has been farmed for its pelt, they are not hunted by people on a significant scale. Some water voles are trapped for their fur in Russia, while Eskimos have traditionally caught collared lemmings in winter and used their white fur for trimming garments. Without a major market for these pelts, however, hunting is never likely to pose much threat to the populations of these animals.

ALTERED STATES

Voles and lemmings can, however, be vulnerable to indirect threats. Their survival in a locality can be seriously affected by pollution in the case of the aquatic species and, most importantly, by changes made to their habitats.

Habitat alteration affects animals in many ways. It can change the amount of vegetation cover available, the food supply, the nature of the soil for burrowing, and the relative abundance of predators. Disturbance and small-scale habitat disruption can cause individual voles or lemmings to abandon former haunts. But if habitat change is widespread

or the amount of suitable habitat too restricted, the animals may have nowhere to retreat and the population in that locality will simply die out.

TIPPING THE BALANCE

In recent decades, intensification in the use of farmland and the increased conversion of land to built-up form has tipped the balance against the majority of species. Mechanization, agrochemicals, and hedgerow removal have taken away much of the remaining cover for voles in European farmland. Increased farming across the western steppes of Ukraine, Russia, and Kazakhstan has caused steppe lemmings to decline. Water voles have declined in parts of their range because of water pollution, riverbank modification, and the removal of waterside

The bank vole enjoys eating berries (right). *But the future supply of this food source depends on hedgerows being left undisturbed.*

Tom McHugh/Oxford Scientific Films

A collared lemming in its summer coat (above) *swimming in Canada; in winter its coat is white.*

Cameron Read/Planet Earth Pictures

This map gives some indiciation of how the distribution of the Norway lemming expands during migration years.

DISTRIBUTION
IN MIGRATION

NORMAL
DISTRIBUTION

Lemming migrations take place about every two to five years, causing the populations to become temporarily much more widely distributed. Naturalists disagree about why lemmings migrate—spring floods, shortage of food, and overcrowding seem to be the chief causes. A year or more of mild weather provides ample vegetation, which encourages abnormally successful breeding and survival and eventually forces the lemmings to seek new territory. A typical journey is only about 10 miles (16 km), but there are reports of lemmings traveling over 280 miles (450 km), from Finland to Russia.

plants, and the muskrat has suffered both from pollution, which can weaken its general health, and from water level regulation, which affects aquatic vegetation, in some lakes of the United States.

Many voles and lemmings, therefore, have undergone a general decline overall. But they remain widely distributed and, where suitable habitat exists, are still abundant. These species are not in any danger of extinction. The same cannot be said, however, for those voles and lemmings with restricted ranges. The Bavarian pine vole, which has not been seen since 1962, may already be extinct. Its only certain habitat—a damp meadow in southern Germany—was destroyed by the construction of a hospital. The white-footed vole, one

ALONGSIDE MAN

THE GREAT ESCAPE

In the early 20th century the muskrat became one of the most important animals in the international fur trade. The animal's dense, soft underfur yields a material that is durable and waterproof, and of such commercial value that up to ten million skins have been harvested in North America in a single year.

Fur farms for the muskrat were also established in central Europe, and it was in 1905 that the first escapees began to establish themselves there in the wild. Finding waterside habitats easily fitting their needs, the feral animals then spread steadily through the continent, reaching across most of northern and eastern Europe.

© Rich Kirchner/NHPA

of the tree voles, is restricted to alder woods along watercourses in coastal Oregon.

A number of other species that have limited distributions are in a vulnerable position. They could easily die out if their restricted habitats are degraded in the future. They include the Balkan snow vole from the mountains of former Yugoslavia; the Tatra pine vole from an area of the Carpathian Mountains in eastern Europe; the beach vole of Muskeget Island, Massachusetts; a vole discovered in 1978 and known only from the Muja River valley in Siberia; and a species that lives only on Mount Zempoaltepec in southern Mexico.

Muskrats can devastate crops, and their digging often damages river and canal banks. They remain pests in Europe, especially in the low-lying Netherlands, where they undermine dykes and dams and create flooding risks.

Even when a species itself is not threatened, it is important to recognize that distinct races or populations of the species may be in danger of dying out. The tundra vole, for instance, has a healthy status across most of northern Eurasia, but many populations of the animal in the western fringes of its range—in, for example, Sweden, Norway, the Netherlands, and Hungary—are now isolated and susceptible to habitat loss. The United States has several similar

---

THE RANGE OF THE HUALAPAI MEXICAN VOLE HAS NOW BEEN REDUCED TO LESS THAN AN ACRE (HALF A HECTARE) OF LAND, WHICH IS HEAVILY GRAZED BY CATTLE

---

cases. Isolated races of the southern bog lemming, each confined to single swamplands in Kansas, Nebraska, and Virginia/North Carolina, face threats from land drainage. The Amargosa vole, a race of the Californian vole that lives only in some marshland near Death Valley, still survives in small numbers but is threatened by possible land development.

RECENT DISCOVERY

The Florida salt marsh vole is a recently discovered race of the meadow vole. It lives in isolation from its fellow grassland-dwellers in a single patch of salt marsh on the Gulf Coast of Florida. It copes with the rising tides by taking refuge in tall vegetation. Having survived in this unusual home perhaps for thousands of years, it now faces the ever-present threat of being wiped out by habitat destruction. ■

VOLES IN DANGER

THE CHART BELOW SHOWS HOW THE INTERNATIONAL UNION FOR THE CONSERVATION OF NATURE (IUCN), OR WORLD CONSERVATION UNION, CLASSIFIES THE STATUS OF VOLES:

BAVARIAN PINE VOLE	EXTINCT (1990)
AMARGOSA VOLE	ENDANGERED (1990)
HUALAPAI MEXICAN VOLE	ENDANGERED (1990)
FLORIDA SALT MARSH VOLE	ENDANGERED (1990)
BEACH VOLE	RARE (1990)

EXTINCT MEANS THAT THE ANIMAL HAS NOT BEEN DEFINITELY LOCATED IN THE WILD DURING THE PAST FIFTY YEARS. ENDANGERED MEANS THAT THE ANIMAL IS IN DANGER OF EXTINCTION AND ITS SURVIVAL IS UNLIKELY UNLESS STEPS ARE TAKEN TO SAVE IT. RARE MEANS THAT THE ANIMAL IS AT RISK, ALTHOUGH NOT AT PRESENT VULNERABLE OR ENDANGERED.

M. C. Wilkes/Aquila

INTO THE FUTURE

Most countries that contain endangered species or populations of voles and lemmings have taken legal steps to prevent people from causing the animals direct harm. But it is the preservation of habitats that is the key to securing the animals' survival. For those species and populations isolated in single sites, the issue is plain.

Unless the coastal home of the Florida salt marsh vole and the marshes haunted by the Amargosa vole are protected against development and disturbance, these animals will slip into extinction in the wild. In such cases, the most effective way to conserve the fragment of suitable habitat is to set the area aside as a nature preserve. The justification for doing so is bolstered by the fact that an isolated wild land, such as a marsh, is likely to be a vital refuge not just for its rodent inhabitants but for other scarce fauna and flora associated with the habitat.

PREDICTION

SECURE PROTECTION

The decline of the outlying European populations of the tundra vole and the steppe lemmings is likely to continue. In the United States, the future of those severely restricted in range will hang in the balance unless their habitats can be securely protected.

For voles and lemmings in general, the most effective way to keep local numbers healthy is to leave "room" for them in the landscape. Some species are already benefiting in some localities by people's growing determination to restore wild spaces settled countryside and even in urban landscapes.

Maintaining hedgerows, unplowed corners, and rough field edges provides food and cover for voles in arable farmland. Leaving patches of land lightly grazed helps voles in pastoral settings, while a scrubby vacant lot in a town can provide habitat for a variety of rodents. In all cases, decreased use of herbicides and poisons will give the animals a better chance of survival.

Once again, of course, the same wild spaces help a whole range of plants and animals. And because voles and lemmings are so important in the food chain, boosting their numbers is vital for the conservation of scarce predators such as the barn owl, hen harrier, wildcat, and pine marten. ∎

THE LONE AFRICAN VOLE

On the Cyrenaica Plateau of northeast Libya and the adjacent coastal plain lives a small, brown rodent, unremarkable but for the fact that it is the only vole in the entire continent of Africa. Its toehold on the continent is a landscape of rocky slopes, cornfields, and a beachside plain vegetated with grasses and shrubs. Known as the Cyrenaica vole, the animal is probably a race of Gunther's vole of Greece and the Middle East—an animal at home in warm, shrubby Mediterranean-type habitats. It is probably a relict population —the product of an ice-age expansion in the species' range when damper climates spread into the Sahara. Voles were left behind in the only part of the coastline where the shrubby Mediterranean habitat persisted, in and around the Cyrenaica Plateau, when the climate became hotter and dryer again. Today the area is isolated in the midst of desert. Should its habitat be degraded by grazing or development, the Cyrenaica vole would have nowhere to retreat.

DINING AT THE TABLE

As for birds, artificial feeding tables can be provided for voles and other rodents, helping them survive in and around towns and villages and offering people a chance to see the wild mammals close up. A wooden board about the size of a small table can be turned into a safe feeding cage by stapling over it a covering of wire mesh supported on corner struts some 24 in (60 cm) high. If the holes in the mesh are about 1 in (2.5 cm) wide, voles can readily slip into the cage, but most predators (including cats) are barred. One side of the cage should be embedded in thick grass or bushes with dense undergrowth so that the rodents can enter under cover. Other cover, such as logs and moss, should be placed inside. Food, such as grain, nuts, and fruit, can be placed in the cage through a securely fastenable wire flap.

Illustration Steve Kingston

WEASELS

RELATIONS

Weasels and polecats belong to the mammal order Carnivora and the family Mustelidae. Other members of the family include:

MINKS

MARTENS

SKUNKS

OTTERS

BADGERS

WOLVERINE

GIANT-SLAYERS

THE WEASELS AND POLECATS ARE THE MOST MURDEROUSLY EFFICIENT OF THE CARNIVORES. A WEASEL CAN KILL AN ANIMAL TEN TIMES ITS SIZE WITH A SINGLE STRIKE, MOVING FASTER THAN THE EYE CAN SEE

Blink and you miss it. A weasel, streaking across the road and vanishing into the grass. Long, sharp, and impossibly slender, like an animated pencil. A blur of chestnut, a flash of white, gone.

A weasel is tiny. It is traditionally capable of slipping its whole body through a wedding ring, and it has evolved that way because squeezing through small gaps is its business. Weasels are burrow hunters: The small weasels take the small game—the mice and voles—while the larger polecats and ferrets tackle the bigger prey. Yet even the biggest polecat is a slender beast compared to a buck rabbit, and the least weasel is the smallest member of the carnivore order. Although small, they are extremely effective.

Typically denizens of the prairie grasslands, many polecats and ferrets have specialized in hunting relatively large, often colonial burrowers such as ground squirrels. The European polecat is more of an opportunist, and its talent for catching

The larger polecats need more space, and the steppe and prairie hunters among them have suffered from the exploitation of their grassland habitats. The marbled polecat, for example, is declining in many areas of central Asia as the steppes are plowed for cereal crops.

In North America the black-footed ferret flourished among the prairie dog colonies of the midwest until farmers and ranchers attempted the elimination of the prairie dog from their lands—an attempt that virtually annihilated the black-footed ferret, if not the prairie dog.

Other species such as the European polecat are less dependent on open grassland, preferring scrub and woodland edge where there is plenty of cover and varied prey; this species in particular is an opportunist that will take anything from earthworms to hares, and this flexibility has enabled it to thrive throughout much of Europe, where the environment has been heavily exploited by man for centuries. Similarly flexible habits have allowed the skunk-striped zorilla to exploit a wide range of habitats across Africa south of the Sahara.

Some of the more obscure weasels show a distinct preference for waterside habitats, an example being the tropical weasel of the Amazon Basin, which is normally seen in association with rivers

Wayne Lankinen/Aquila

FOCUS ON

LAPLAND

In Lapland the snow glows an eerie blue in the 24-hour gloom of the arctic winter. It is a barren scene, yet beneath the snow there is life. Insulated from the icy winds above, voles and lemmings scuttle through runways, digging for roots and nibbling the buried vegetation, while creeping behind come the sleek, white shapes of the stoats and weasels that prey on them.

These northern weasels are ideally adapted for hunting small rodents under the snow, having abandoned any attempt at living on the snow surface in favor of a burrowing lifestyle that enables them to avoid the worst of the arctic climate altogether. Both stoats and weasels adapt coats of pure white to make them less visible to eyes in the sky on their rare excursions above ground.

The stoats and weasels of Lapland are actually smaller than the weasels of warmer regions to the south, because this enables them to penetrate the lemming runs more easily and they can rely on the snow cover to keep them warm. Being smaller also reduces the amount of food they need, which is useful in years when prey is scarce. In the opposite situation, when lemmings undergo the massive population explosions for which they are notorious, both weasels and stoats are able to breed rapidly to exploit the bonanza.

TEMPERATURE AND RAINFALL

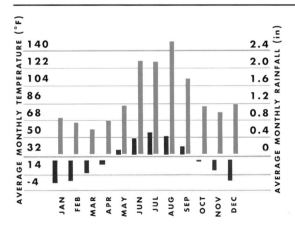

■ TEMPERATURE

■ RAINFALL

The chart shows the temperature and rainfall for Inari, in the northernmost reaches of Finland. Here winter lasts from October to early May, with periods of permanent darkness. During the brief summer, daylight lasts around the clock.

and streams. Its feet are partially webbed, as are those of the closely related Colombian weasel, suggesting a semiaquatic lifestyle like that of the mink. Meanwhile the North African banded weasel lives in arid regions on the fringes of the Sahara, where it burrows into sand dunes to escape the scorching heat of the day. The contrast with the tiny least weasel of the north, which burrows into the snow to escape the numbing cold, illustrates the remarkable adaptability of this hugely successful group of carnivores. ■

NEIGHBORS

Lying well within the Arctic Circle, Lapland is the largest wilderness in western Europe. Despite its harsh, long winters, it provides a haven for wildlife—both the summer visitors and year-round residents.

PEREGRINE

On the tundra the peregrine is free of the pesticides that almost eliminated it from much of Europe.

VIVIPAROUS LIZARD

The only lizard found within the Arctic Circle, this species spends the winter dormant beneath the snow.

Neighbor illustrations Joanne Cowne. Owl by Elisabeth Smith

THE ROOF OF EUROPE
In the far north of Scandinavia lies Lapland, a remote wilderness of dark coniferous forests, lakes, moorland, and mountain tundra. The whole region lies north of the Arctic Circle, and for much of the year the landscape lies under deep snow.

Barents Sea

Arctic Circle

SWEDEN

FINLAND

LAPLAND

WOLF

Large packs still survive in the northern wildernesses, although they are often shot by Lapp reindeer herders.

HARE

The hare's white winter camouflage may not provide sufficient protection against persistent predators.

SNOWY OWL

Although it preys mainly on lemmings, the superb snowy owl is a major threat to stoats and weasels.

COMMON FROG

The common frog is one of the few amphibians capable of thriving in the far north. It is often preyed upon by stoats.

NORWAY LEMMING

The lemmings' population booms and crashes affect the survival of the predators that depend on them.

HUNTING

Being a predator is a high-risk business. While herbivores consume low-value foods in quantity and spend most of their lives eating placidly, carnivores go for quality and spend most of their lives in a state of stress, either through the dangers of hunting or the threat of starvation. Some prey animals are easy to find but well defended, forcing predators to select either the weaklings or to hunt cooperatively to overcome the prey's defenses. Other prey animals are easy to kill but often hard to find, forcing predators to forage for hours on empty stomachs. Such prey is often small—which is why it is easy to kill—and this encourages a predator to hunt alone. It also has to repeat the process many times if it is to get enough to eat; in such circumstances it risks using more energy than it acquires and eventually succumbing to starvation.

SOLITARY SEARCHERS

Many predators will take both kinds of prey at different times and seasons, but most veer toward one strategy or the other. The weasels and polecats are essentially solitary searchers, spending a lot more time looking for prey than attacking and killing it. They rarely hunt as teams, and even when several immature brothers and sisters forage together—as happens among stoats, for example—they do not employ the sophisticated tactics of professional pack hunters like wolves or lions. Even large, powerful prey animals, such as jackrabbits and hares, are attacked alone, often at considerable risk: A lucky kick from a hare could kill a stoat. Accordingly, most species concentrate on prey that lies well within their capabilities and tackle larger animals only occasionally.

BURROW-HUNTING SPECIALISTS

The tendency to pick on prey their own size also helps to divide the resources among different species living in the same region. Most weasels and polecats are specialized burrow hunters and, by limiting their activities to burrows that they fit snugly, each species—and even each sex—can secure a virtual monopoly of its prey. In Ontario, for example, the local race of stoat is compact enough to hunt voles in their runs beneath the snow. The females, being smaller, are particularly well equipped for the job, and this may ensure that they secure enough nourishment for breeding. Meanwhile the long-tailed weasel is too big to hunt

Anthony Bannister/NHPA

A native of Africa's semiarid regions, the skunklike zorilla feeds on its rodent prey.

voles under the snow, but it is perfectly proportioned for entering the wider tunnels of water voles, ground squirrels, and rabbits. It is also powerful enough to make short work of the occupants while incurring minimal risk to itself, whereas a small female stoat entering the same tunnels would run a greater risk of injury.

In Europe, vole hunting, whether in grass or snow, is the speciality of the common weasel, while the stoat—larger than its Canadian counterpart—concentrates on rabbits and water voles. Both species will take other prey, however, including mice, rats, frogs, lizards, and birds, but they normally avoid shrews, which appear to have an unpleasant taste. The European polecat takes a similar range of prey but is more opportunist in its approach; it is less of a burrow specialist than the smaller species. By contrast, other polecat species have become dedicated to a particular type of prey: The black-footed ferret, for example, feeds exclusively on prairie dogs and lives within their tunnel systems. ■

SCARED TO DEATH
Paralyzed by fright, a rabbit may not need much killing (left). "Stoated" rabbits have been known to drop dead of heart failure, quite unmarked.

in SIGHT

SURPLUS KILLING

Weasels and polecats are strongly conditioned to store surplus food, since they never know from where their next meal is coming. If a weasel comes across a large colony of mice, for example, it may kill 30–40 of them and cache them for later. Obviously this habit is of limited value in warm weather because the carcasses decay rapidly, but in a cold climate—which several weasels have evolved to exploit— they could form the basis of a very useful cold food store.

This caching habit may be the origin of the "surplus killing" tendency that has made these animals notorious among poultry farmers and gamekeepers. If a weasel or polecat manages to penetrate a pheasant breeding pen, for example, it will keep killing until all the chicks are dead or until it is exhausted.

Color illustration Kim Thompson

THE LETHAL STAB
Terror tactics may work in some cases, but normally the killer delivers the deathblow in the conventional fashion. In the smaller species the strike can be lightning fast—a swift lunge to the back of the neck and a lethal stab with the canines (left).

PINNING ITS PREY
Often a weasel will pinion its prey by wrapping its long body around it before going for the kill, yet the whole business is usually over within a minute (left).

TERRITORY

Weasels and polecats are not sociable animals. For much of the year their main preoccupation is finding food, and they take little notice of their mustelid neighbors. Their prey requirements dictate how much terrain they cover on a regular basis—the home range—and the area involved can vary greatly depending on the prey available in the habitat. In Wales, where prey is plentiful, the local European polecats range over an average of 250 acres (100 ha), but in Russia polecats are known to occupy home ranges of up to 6,200 acres (2,500 ha).

The maximum range of the polecat is disproportionately bigger than that of the stoat because it takes larger prey that is relatively scarce. This disadvantage of large size may explain why the female of each species tends to be smaller than the male, since it allows her to get all the prey she needs for herself and her young within a relatively confined area. The sexes are tolerant toward each other, but they will not tolerate intruders of the same sex. A male defends his patch against neighboring males, while a female defends hers against other females.

The effectiveness of this defense depends on the area involved. A polecat with an extensive home range cannot patrol its boundaries on a daily basis, and there is bound to be a good deal of trespassing. Smaller ranges are easier to police, but even so most animals tend to be casual at the limits of their

SCENT MARKING

Weasels defend their hunting grounds vigorously by drenching the area in urine, feces, and powerful-smelling secretions from the anal scent gland.

DIVIDING THE SPOILS

The large territories of male weasels and polecats often encompass the smaller territories of several females, even though the males—and the females—avoid sharing terrain with others of the same sex. In the breeding season this arrangement is obviously to the advantage of the male, but what about the rest of the year?

The two sexes can afford to live like this because they are different sizes. A female weasel is only half the size of a male, so she can enter smaller burrows and take smaller prey. Meanwhile the male, being more powerful, can concentrate on bigger prey, and since larger animals tend to be scarcer he has to range farther to find them; hence the larger territory. In this way the sexes can divide the spoils between them.

■■■■ MALE

▬ ▬ ▬ FEMALE

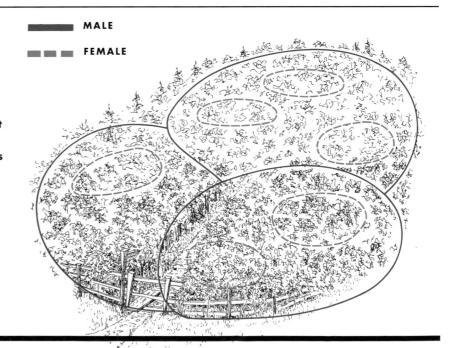

B/W illustration Ruth Grewcock

MATERNITY RULES

Mostly, might is right for weasels and polecats, with the dominant individual in any region usually being the biggest male. But the hierarchy in some species, such as the stoat, changes dramatically when the females become pregnant, for the expectant mothers achieve a status comparable with that of the big males. This helps them extend and defend their feeding territories, which are obviously vital during this period, and when the young are born it assures a good supply of milk and a measure of security against rogue males that might be tempted to cannibalism.

Color illustration Jacqui Harper/Wildlife Art Agency

them that they are on dangerous ground and they will beat a retreat.

The scent is quite individual. Another weasel or polecat of the same species encountering a scent mark can tell the sex, sexual condition, and identity of the individual that left it. For although these animals are not highly social, they do have distinct dominance hierarchies.

During the breeding season, however, things change somewhat. Males may travel way beyond their usual ranges, presumably in search of receptive females. The range of a dominant stoat, for example, may increase fiftyfold. ∎

ranges and only get seriously proprietorial about the "core areas"—the favored hunting grounds where they spend most of their time.

Territory defense is largely psychological, based on the pungent power of scent. A weasel or polecat will take care to leave its scent wherever it goes—in the form of urine or droppings or secretions from its anal scent glands—and the more frequently an area is visited, the more drenched in scent it becomes. The effect is partly accidental, but an animal will often deliberately smear its scent on the terrain by dragging its rear end along the ground. It may also rub its throat on prominent objects to deposit scent from another set of glands. These scents have a reassuring effect on the territory holder and a distinctly discouraging effect on any trespassers that, surrounded by alien smells, are usually seen off by the confident resident. Most intruders, indeed, rarely get this far; the evidence of their noses tells

A polecat emerges from its den. The den's former occupant may have been evicted or eaten.

Rolf Bender/Frank Lane Picture Agency

REPRODUCTION

Compared to larger carnivores such as dogs and bears, all weasels and polecats are fast breeders. The smaller they are, the faster they breed: A female least weasel is sexually mature at three months and is likely to breed in her first summer. She may also have a second litter later in the year, by which time the females in her first litter may themselves be breeding. Since a least weasel averages six kits in each litter, she has the potential to generate 30 descendants in her first year of life: two litters of six each, plus a brood of six apiece from the three daughters in her first litter (her male offspring are unlikely to breed quite so rapidly).

THE PACE OF LIFE

This cracking pace is partly a consequence of the least weasel's fast metabolism. This animal races through life and is generally dead within the year; as a result everything happens quickly. A fast metabolism is not the sole reason for fast breeding, however. Like all animals, the weasels and polecats have developed breeding strategies that are defined partly by biological constraints such as metabolic rate and partly by the circumstances in which they live. In the case of the least weasel, evolution has tailored it to exploit the burrowing rodents of the tundra: the voles and lemmings. For reasons that are not entirely clear, these animals undergo roughly four-year cycles of population boom and crash: On any acre of Alaskan tundra the brown lemming population may proliferate to 100 or more, crash to less than a couple within two years, then build up to 100 again. Such wild fluctuations favor

Steve Downer/Aquila

A polecat-ferret with her young. Albinos and white or pale fur are common among ferrets.

predators that can match the pace by breeding rapidly to exploit temporary gluts in the prey supply, and the least weasel fits this specification perfectly.

The stoat also hunts on the tundra, and although its slower metabolism prevents it from breeding quite as fast as the common or least weasel, it has developed a couple of tricks that help it make the most of "lemming years." The first is the disposable litter. An ovulating female produces an average of

BIRTH BURROW

A stoat with her young in an underground burrow (below). The babies are born blind and covered with fine down. Their eyes open at five to six weeks, and they are fully furred at about eight weeks.

Color illustrations Peter David Scott/Wildlife Art Agency

LEAVING HOME

When young weasels and polecats reach the age of independence, they tend to move away to find feeding territories of their own. Females do not move as far as males, and among a population of stoats studied in Sweden, the immature females tended to settle on or near their mothers' territories. Among such short-lived species, the female often dies within a few months of giving birth, enabling one of her daughters to inherit her territory.

In the Swedish study, the males tended to linger in their mothers' territories throughout the autumn and winter, then set off on extensive travels.

ten eggs, and in a poor year most of these are either not fertilized, are aborted, or die at the suckling stage. Only the strongest survive, and ultimately this is to the good of the species. In a "lemming year," however, when the tundra is teeming with prey, the extra nutrition enables the mother to bring all the embryos to term, suckle them all, and rear them all to take advantage of the abundant food supplies.

The other trick involves delayed implantation, in which the true gestation starts several months after mating. This in itself is of little value, but the female stoat capitalizes on it by mating while she is still a suckling infant—often with the male that has just mated with her mother. Hormones in the mother's milk probably activate her daughters' reproductive systems to make this possible. The development of the young female's litter is delayed until early spring, when she is old enough to bear young and when the lemmings are just starting to multiply.

MATING AND BIRTH

Courtship and mating are rough and prolonged in weasels and polecats. This is because ovulation is triggered by the mating act, and if it is over too quickly, ovulation may not be activated. The male has a well-developed penis bone or baculum, which he uses to good purpose while grabbing the female by the neck with his sharp teeth and dragging her around; a polecat will often draw blood. The whole

ON THE MOVE

If threatened or if hunting is bad, the mother will move her young, carrying them by the scruff of the neck.

HIGH JINKS

Adolescent polecats play-fighting (below).

business lasts for up to an hour in the case of polecats; captive black-footed ferrets may keep going for up to three and a half hours.

The kits are born blind and covered in fine down. For the first few weeks they are totally dependent on their mother, who rears them alone, without any assistance from the male. This can be hard work, for once they are weaned—at three to six weeks in common weasels—she has to keep them supplied with freshly killed prey; the small size of the female can be a mixed blessing here, since although it reduces her own food requirements, it also puts a limit on the size of prey she can carry back to the nest. At six to eight weeks, young weasels can kill their own prey, but they generally hunt in family groups for some weeks before branching out on their own; this enables them to polish up their predatory skills and sometimes overpower relatively large animals that they would be rash to tackle alone. ∎

KEEPING A LOW PROFILE

ALTHOUGH TRAPPED FOR THEIR FUR AND WIDELY REVILED AS VERMIN, MOST WEASELS AND POLECATS STILL FLOURISH IN THE WILD THANKS TO THEIR ADAPTABILITY, OPPORTUNISM, AND ABILITY TO KEEP OUT OF SIGHT

For thousands of years weasels and polecats have flourished in a variety of habitats through a combination of special adaptations and opportunism. The adaptations have enabled them to hunt burrowing animals in their tunnels, giving them access to a prey resource that other carnivores cannot exploit. Meanwhile, their opportunism has enabled them to hunt new prey in new regions, allowing them to colonize environments that are quite unlike those in which they evolved.

STOATS DOWN UNDER

The stoat, for example, probably evolved as a specialist predator of water voles. These often occur far from water and dig burrows that are tailor-made for stoats. Across much of continental Europe, water voles are still high on the stoat's menu, but in Great Britain they are now scarce, and the local stoats prey mainly on rabbits. This talent for rabbit catching inspired the farmers of New Zealand to import several stoats from Great Britain in the 19th century and free them on their rabbit-plagued pastures; since then the stoats have prospered in a land where most of their "normal" prey species are unknown. Instead, they eat rabbits—although less than one might expect—birds of all kinds, introduced rats and mice, insects, brush-tailed opossums (introduced from Australia), lizards, crayfish, and carrion. Their feeding habits are unlike those of European stoats, particularly with respect to the quantity of insects in their diet. This is partly because New Zealand boasts some especially large and nutritious insects such as the giant weta, a type of outsized cricket. So stoats have come a long way from water voles and have shown a remarkable capacity for survival in a strange land.

A number of common weasels were introduced to New Zealand along with the stoats, but they have not flourished in the same way, possibly because there are relatively few small mammals for them to prey upon. Elsewhere, however, their talents for living in tight corners and breeding rapidly to exploit new prey resources has served them well, and they have spread into a huge variety of habitats across the Northern Hemisphere. They have been

Joy Langsbury/Bruce Coleman Ltd.

Many farmers are convinced that the only good polecat is a dead polecat (above).

Hans Reinhard/Bruce Coleman Ltd.

 OUT OF ACTION

DEADLY WORMS

The smaller weasels are plagued by a parasitic nematode worm that infests the nasal sinuses of the skull. The worms form tight knots and, either by pressure or through the secretion of some corrosive substance, gradually distort the skull bones and may even cause holes to appear in the cranium. The worms have a highly complex life cycle. In time, they produce larvae that pass out of the weasel in its feces; the larvae are picked up by snails, where they develop into an intermediate stage. If the snail is then eaten by a mouse or vole, which is by no means uncommon, and the mouse or vole is devoured by a weasel, the worm gets to complete its life cycle.

The skull damage caused by these worms is so severe that it must have some effect on the weasel's health. So far there is no proof that the parasite actually causes death or serious debility, but the pressure exerted by the swelling on the brain may cause irritation, pain, or even some mental malfunction. It is possible that the legendary weasel "dances," in which the animals cavort in full view of their prey and sometimes catch and kill their bemused spectators, are not deliberate hunting ploys but involuntary, temporary fits brought on by parasite infestation.

highly successful on farmland, where they find rich pickings in the fields, hedgerows, and farmyards. By destroying mice and other vermin, they have probably made a major contribution to farm profits over the centuries, but this has not stopped man from regarding weasels—as well as stoats, polecats, and other small mustelids—as vermin themselves.

THE GAMEKEEPERS' SCOURGE

The problem is that many wild carnivores simply cannot resist attacking domestic livestock. Confined at high density, such animals are sitting targets for predators, and since weasels and other predators often kill far more than they need for food, the losses can be dramatic. Stoats and polecats often attack poultry, but more dangerously—in terms of retaliation—they also raid game-bird breeding pens and

Stoats can wreak havoc in poultry pens, wantonly slaughtering birds and stealing their eggs.

ALONGSIDE MAN

THE DOMESTIC FERRET

The ferret has been domesticated for at least 2,000 years. Aristotle described it in the fourth century B.C., but it may have been known in Palestine before 1000 B.C. Its skull resembles that of the steppe polecat, but its chromosomes are identical to those of the European polecat, enabling it to interbreed and produce fertile hybrids. These hybrids look a lot like wild polecats.

The history of the ferret is inextricably mixed up with that of the rabbit, which has also been domesticated for centuries as a source of food. The rabbits were traditionally kept in enclosed warrens and flushed out as required by introducing a ferret at one end of the burrow system and netting the rabbits as they bolted from the exits. The method is still used to flush wild rabbits, although today the rabbits are often shot rather than netted. The ferret will usually be muzzled, for if it catches one it is likely to stay underground to eat it, forcing its owner to dig it out. Albino ferrets are often favored for their visibility in the dark, making them easier to locate when they are missing, but many are never found.

have demonstrated their ability to adapt to new environments, but many tropical species may be less capable of exploiting new opportunities. We know so little about many of these species that we cannot afford to be optimistic, and several are assumed to be under threat simply because their native wildernesses are being destroyed.

Meanwhile, populations of the larger polecats are definitely suffering: The steppe polecat and marbled polecat of southeastern Europe, central Asia, and China are retreating in the face of agricultural "reclamation" of the steppe grasslands, and the black-footed ferret of the American prairies has been plucked from the jaws of extinction only by a captive-breeding program. This particular species may yet be reintroduced successfully to the prairie dog colonies it evolved to exploit, but its future will depend on man's toleration rather than the animal's natural talent for survival, which seems built into some of its smaller relatives. ■

Lithe, sinuous, and deadly, ferrets are still used today to flush rabbits from their warrens.

Ian Beames/Ardea

INTO THE FUTURE

Compared to most carnivores, weasels and polecats are generally well equipped to face the future. Most species can thrive in small patches of suitable habitat and are elusive enough to escape notice. Their principal human enemies, the game-keepers and fur trappers, are either dwindling in numbers or changing their tactics. The number of gamekeepers in Great Britain has fallen by 80 percent this century, and many of those that remain would rather be custodians of wildlife than indiscriminate killers of all predators. In the northern fur-trapping regions, the economic justi-fication for taking ermine has become tenuous. This is partly because preparing 300 pelts for a single coat is a tedious and costly task, and partly because the idea of wearing the pelts of 300 dead animals has become repellent to many people.

The problem of habitat loss may also be easing

PREDICTION

CONCERN FOR THE SPECIALISTS

Local extinctions are commonplace among small weasels, but these adaptable animals can rapidly make up the losses. The more specialized, slower breeding species are less resilient, and we must make sure that they are not put to the test.

in some areas. In Europe a fair amount of marginal farmland is being allowed to go back to the wild, creating large areas of prime habitat for burrowing rodents and, by extension, for weasels and polecats. Rabbit numbers have soared over the last decade, almost up to the plague proportions experienced before the species was almost annihilated by the myxomatosis epidemic of the 1950s. This is bad news for farmers but good news for stoats and pole-cats: The stoats suffered badly during the rabbit famine and are flourishing today.

Elsewhere in the world the future of weasels and polecats is less sure. Several species have lost their wild habitats and may not be able to adapt to farmed landscapes as their European counterparts have done. Many are opportunist predators, with the adaptability that this implies. Some, however, may have specialized requirements, like the black-footed ferret of North America, and may suffer a similar fate. ∎

Illustration Mark Stewart/Wildlife Art Agency

BLACK-FOOTS AT LARGE

In 1992, 49 captive-bred black-footed ferrets were released near a large prairie dog town in Wyoming, after an acclimatization period during which they were hand-fed on the prairie. The animals were radio-collared, enabling them to be tracked from six tracking stations placed around the release site. Since dispersal is the most dangerous phase of a wild ferret's life, the zoologists expected a high mortality rate, and the released animals represented only a small percentage of the captive population. Some have been killed by coyotes, but at least a quarter have survived for long enough to convince the scientists that captive breeding and release is a viable proposition, and that black-footed ferrets may once again become established in the wild.

GRAY WHALES

RELATIONS

Gray whales belong to the whale and dolphin order, Cetacea, and to the suborder Mysticeti, or baleen whales. Other mysticetes include:

BLUE WHALE

HUMPBACK WHALE

RIGHT WHALE

BOWHEAD WHALE

MINKE WHALE

SEI WHALE

FIN WHALE

BRYDE'S WHALE

François Gohier/Ardea

FAMILIAR, YET MYSTERIOUS

THE GRAY WHALE IS ONE OF THE MOST WATCHED AND TOUCHED OF ALL WHALES, YET FUNDAMENTAL QUESTIONS ABOUT ITS EVOLUTION AND RELATIONSHIPS ARE STILL UNANSWERED

T he world center for whale-watching is the Pacific coast of North America— from the shallow, subtropical lagoons along the coasts of Mexico, California, Oregon, and Washington to British Columbia and Alaska. This is the route that the gray whales swim each spring, from their southern winter "resorts" to their Arctic summer feeding grounds. The whales return south in autumn, completing the longest regular migration of any mammal on the planet. They

provide the experience of a lifetime for the whale-watchers, who watch from the shore or venture in inflatables and small boats to touch and marvel at these huge, powerful beasts.

The gray whale is a great, or baleen whale: It belongs to the select group of the largest animals on Earth. These vast creatures filter small animals and other items of food from seawater with the sievelike fringes of baleen (whalebone) that hang down from the upper jaws inside the mouth. The baleen of the

The gray whale belongs to the Cetacean order, which includes all whales, dolphins, and porpoises. There are two Cetacean suborders: toothed whales, including the porpoises, dolphins, killer whales, sperm whales, and beaked whales; and baleen whales, which number three species of right whales, six rorqual species, and the gray whale.

ORDER

Cetacea
(whales and dolphins)

SUBORDER

Mysticeti
(baleen whales)

FAMILY

Eschrichtiidae

GENUS AND SPECIES

Eschrichtius robustus

The beaklike jaws (below) *conceal long curtains of baleen, through which the whale sieves its food.*

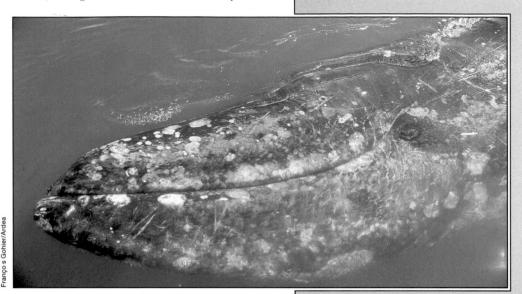

François Gohier/Ardea

great whales distinguishes them from their cousins, the toothed whales, which include dolphins, porpoises, sperm whales, and beaked whales.

There are ten species of baleen whales. Six are rorquals: the humpback, blue, fin, sei, Bryde's, and minke. They are long, slim, and torpedo-shaped, with many grooves or pleats in the skin of their long throats. Three of the baleen whales are right whales: the right whale itself, the pygmy right whale, and the bowhead whale. They have vast mouths almost one-third the length of the body and strongly arched upper jaws from which hangs the longest baleen of any great whale. The tenth species in the baleen group is the gray. For all its familiarity to the peoples of Pacific North America, the gray whale remains a mysterious creature; its relationships with the other great whales are unclear. In fact, it differs from them so greatly that it is put in a separate family all its own—the Eschrichtiidae.

PRIMITIVE, BUT NOT OBSOLETE

In evolutionary terms, the gray is often regarded as the most primitive of the baleen whales. Even its appearance looks prehistoric, a lumpy head with down-turned mouth. The skin of the typical adult gray is heavily colonized by barnacles, lice, and other small residents. Such a profusion of parasites usually indicates that a species has been around, largely unchanged, for perhaps millions of years. Barnacles thrive on the front and top of the whale's head and neck, while whale lice hide in the folds of the eyes, blowholes, and mouth corners. One species of barnacle and three kinds of whale lice are found only on the gray whale. The rudimentary hairs or bristles on the gray whale's skin may

François Gohier/Ardea

in SIGHT

RORQUAL OR RIGHT?

The gray whale is distinctive enough to be given its own family within the baleen whale group, but it has many physical characteristics that seem midway between right whales and rorquals.

The gray is about the length of the right whale, yet not as long as the huge blue and fin whales; its shape is more like the slim rorquals, rather than the wide, bulky rights. Its flukes are longer and narrower than those of the right whales, yet more stubby than those of the rorquals. Rorquals have many throat grooves or pleats—more than 100 in some individuals. The right and bowhead whales have none, while the gray has two, very occasionally four, such throat grooves. The gray's rostrum—its long, beaklike snout—is narrower than that of the rorquals, more like the rostrum of the right whale. Yet it is also gently curved or arched, more like a rorqual than a right.

also be evolutionary leftovers. In other whales, these hairs—the fur of the original land-dwelling mammal ancestor—are virtually absent.

ANCIENT WHALES

The cetaceans—the whales, dolphins and porpoises—probably evolved from the condylarths. These carnivorous, hoofed land mammals that may have resembled large wolves, lived about 60 million years ago. They may have been the ancestors of two main groups: the modern hoofed mammals and the mesonychids (mez-o-NIE-kids). Some mesonychids may have lived on the shore, later evolving into the earliest whales, the Archaeoceti (ar-kee-o-SET-ee). They developed peglike teeth, their forelegs evolved into paddles, and their bodies became long and eel-like, with tail flukes for swimming.

One version of the whales' past holds that there were three groups of Archaeoceti. The Protocetidae (pro-to-SET-id-ie) were the first whalelike creatures from 50 million years ago. They included Pakicetus (pak-ee-SET-us), a small, otterlike animal with long jaws. The second group were the more dolphinlike Dorudontinae, living some 40 million years ago. Third were the Basilosauridae, including Basilosaurus, also from around 40 million years ago. This very whalelike beast had front flippers,

The huge flukes of the tail are the powerhouse of the gray whale, driving it down deep to feed.

and its hind legs had almost disappeared. It may have also had a dorsal fin and tail flukes. The nostrils had started their long evolutionary journey from the front tip of the snout, as in most mammals, up and back to the top of the head, where they now form the blowhole of modern whales. From such an animal as Basilosaurus the toothed whales may have evolved, some 30 million years ago.

Next came the cetotheres (SET-o-theers), the largest family of whales ever, with about 60 species of moderate size. They date from about 25 million years ago. The family peaked in numbers and diversity about 15 million years ago and may have given rise to the modern baleen whales.

EVOLUTIONARY TRENDS

As the baleen whales evolved, the skull and neck were modified for the filter-feeding way of life. The skull and neck bones became pushed or telescoped together and firmly joined, so a whale has no visible external neck and cannot twist its internal neck, either. However, the gray whale has the least telescoped and fused skull and neck bones of all baleen whales. This may be another pointer to its primitive or little-changed status.

There are, however, other versions of the whales' past. It is possible that 38–25 million years ago the Archaeoceti were replaced by four families. Two, the Agorophiidae (ag-o-ro-FIE-id-ie) and Squalodontidae (skwa-lo-DONT-id-ie) were the ancestors of the modern toothed whales. The other two were the Aetiocetidae (ie-tee-o-SET-id-ie) which had teeth, and the Cetotheriidae (cetotheres), which did not; these were the first definite baleen whales. By about 30 million years ago, the teeth had been fully replaced by baleen.

THE GRAYS TODAY

Within recorded history, gray whales were common in both the North Atlantic (including the North Sea) and North Pacific Oceans. Remains of grays have been found in reclaimed land in the Netherlands, Sweden, and East Anglia. It is believed that the Atlantic and North Sea grays became extinct by the 18th century, but perhaps not solely due to early whaling: They were probably always rare. Today, the Atlantic population is completely extinct.

There are two populations or stocks of gray whales in the North Pacific. The very small and extremely endangered one in the west is known as the Korean, Asian, or West Pacific stock. The much larger one in the East Pacific—the subject of so much whale-watching today—is the California or American stock. Both groups migrate north to feed near the Arctic ice during the summer months. ∎

THE GRAY WHALE'S FAMILY TREE

Baleen, or whalebone, is unique in the animal kingdom and separates the great whales from all other mammals. The baleen may have evolved from small fringes along the gums in the roof of the mouth. The gray whale is assigned its own family, distinct from the other great whales, and usually sited somewhere between the rorquals and the right whales.

BLUE WHALE

BALEEN WHALES

SPERM WHALE

TOOTHED WHALES

WHALES & DOLPHINS

GRAY WHALE

Eschrichtius robustus
(*es-KRIK-tee-us ro-BUS-tus*)

The gray is the least typical of the baleen whales and is in many ways more similar to the ancestors of the great whales. Like several other large, dark, ocean creatures, such as the manta ray, the gray is also called the devilfish.

BOWHEAD WHALE

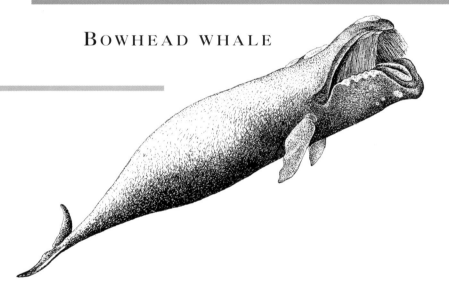

ⒶNCESTORS

AGE-OLD SWIMMERS

Some 15 million years ago, *Cetotherium* (set-o-THEER-ee-um) swam in the seas that covered much of what is now Europe. *Cetotherium* was about 13 ft (4 m) long; from its fossils, it probably resembled a small version of today's gray whale. It may have fed on shrimp, using relatively short baleen plates. Its family, the cetotheres, may have evolved in the late Oligocene period, 30–25 million years ago, as the first of the baleen whales. *Cetotherium* would have been preyed upon by the immense-jawed *Carcharodon* (car-CAR-o-don); at 40 ft (12 m) long, this close relative of today's great white shark was the largest predatory shark that ever lived.

B/W illustrations Ruth Grewcock. Gray whale Richard Tibbitts

DOLPHINS

PORPOISES

ANATOMY:
THE GRAY WHALE

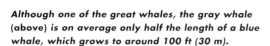

THE BACK

lacks a dorsal fin; instead, a lumpy ridge extends along the rear third or so of its length, with about ten humps that become progressively smaller toward the tail stock.

Although one of the great whales, the gray whale (above) is on average only half the length of a blue whale, which grows to around 100 ft (30 m).

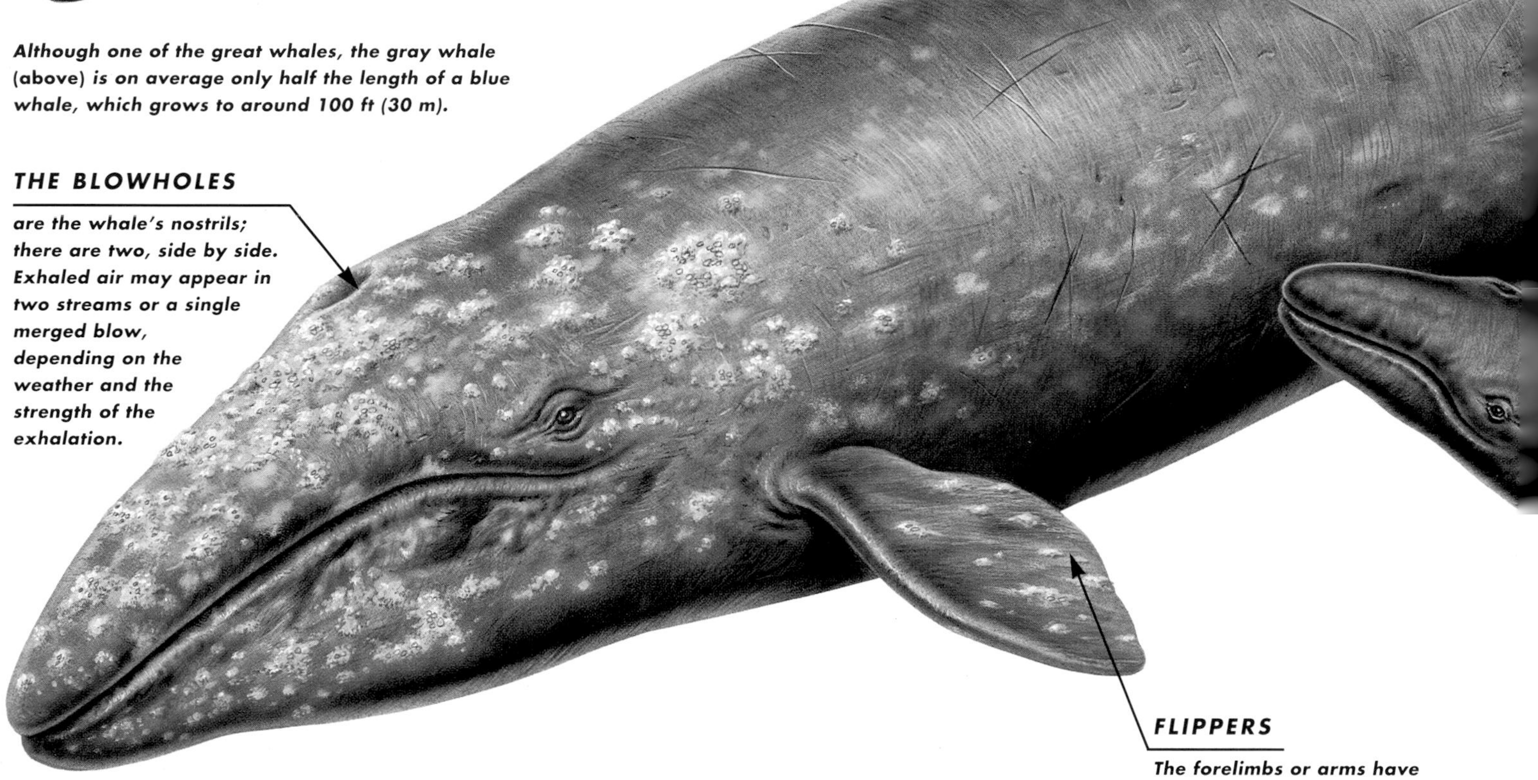

THE BLOWHOLES

are the whale's nostrils; there are two, side by side. Exhaled air may appear in two streams or a single merged blow, depending on the weather and the strength of the exhalation.

SURFACE FEATURES

Most adult grays are encrusted with barnacles and whale lice (right), marked with pale scars from battles with sharks and killer whales, and disfigured with moon-shaped scars caused by the mouths of lampreys and similar bloodsuckers.

FLIPPERS

The forelimbs or arms have become large, rounded pectoral fins, or flippers. These are short and broad, used mainly for steering and for slow, relaxed swimming. They are supported by bones that parallel those in the human arm and hand.

SKELETON

There are no rear limb bones, except tiny leftovers buried in the flesh of the flanks. The tail flukes have no bones inside: They are mainly skin and muscle.

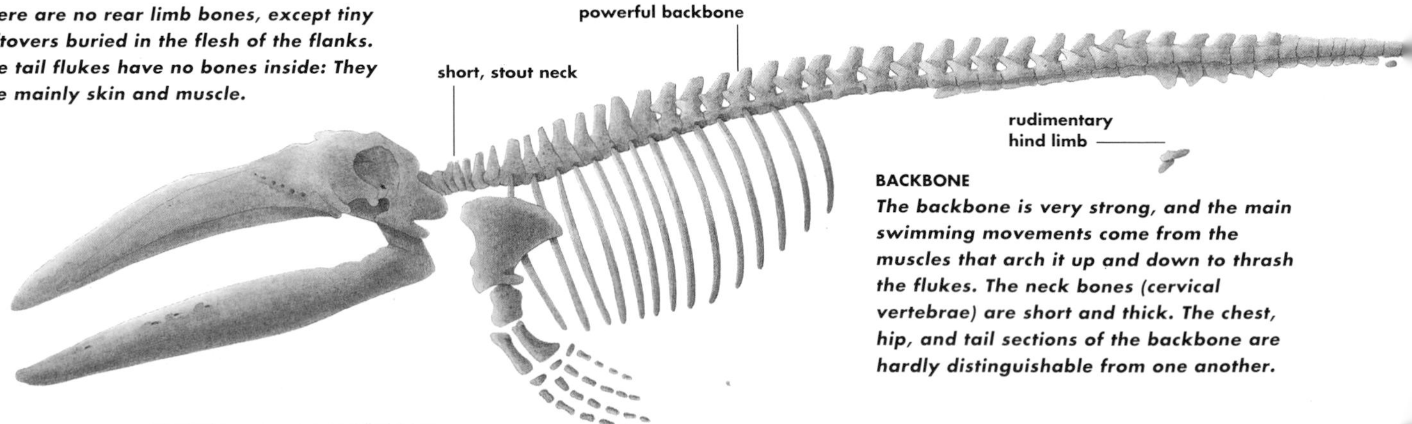

short, stout neck

powerful backbone

rudimentary hind limb

BACKBONE

The backbone is very strong, and the main swimming movements come from the muscles that arch it up and down to thrash the flukes. The neck bones (cervical vertebrae) are short and thick. The chest, hip, and tail sections of the backbone are hardly distinguishable from one another.

X-ray illustrations Elisabeth Smith

DORSAL FINS

KILLER WHALE   **GRAY WHALE**   **HUMPBACK WHALE**

The male orca or killer whale reveals a long, very upright dorsal fin as it surfaces, whereas the gray's back is smooth, except for a few bumps near the tail section. Like most other rorquals, the humpback whale has a low, curved fin.

THE SKIN

becomes calloused by the barnacles that grow into it. The generations of barnacles build up, increasing the thickness of the encrustation. Under the skin is a thick layer of blubbery fat, which helps to hold in body warmth.

THE BABY GRAY

is smooth, sleek, and glistening and shows the true color of the skin before it is discolored by parasites, growths, lumps, and scars.

THE FLUKES

measure over 10 ft (3 m) from tip to tip. They swish up and down powerfully to thrust the whale through the water. They are also used for smacking the surface for signaling.

FACT FILE:

THE GRAY WHALE

CLASSIFICATION

GENUS: *ESCHRICHTIUS*
SPECIES: *ROBUSTUS*

SIZE

TOTAL LENGTH/MALE: 40–45 FT (12–14 M)
TOTAL LENGTH/FEMALE: 43–50 FT (13–15 M)
WEIGHT/MALE: 16.5–27.5 TONS, VARIABLE DEPENDING UPON THE SEASON
WEIGHT/FEMALE: 22–27.5 TONS (33–38.6 TONS WHEN PREGNANT)
LENGTH AT BIRTH: 16.4 FT (5 M)

COLORATION

GENERALLY GRAY, BEING DARKER SLATE GRAY ON THE BACK AND SLIGHTLY PALER ON THE UNDERSIDE
MUCH MOTTLING AND PATCHES OR SCARS CAUSED BY SHARK OR KILLER WHALE BITES AND LAMPREY SUCKERS
SKIN ALSO USUALLY BEARS WHITISH OR YELLOW ENCRUSTATIONS OF BARNACLES, LICE, AND OTHER EXTERNAL PARASITES, ESPECIALLY OVER UPPER HEAD AND ALONG BACK AND FLANKS
RARE WHITISH ALBINO INDIVIDUALS OCCUR

FEATURES

UNIFORM GRAYISH COLORATION ENLIVENED BY EXTERIOR PARASITES SUCH AS LICE AND BARNACLES
NO PROPER DORSAL FIN, BUT A RIDGE ALONG THE REAR THIRD OF THE UPPER BACK WITH ABOUT 9–12 SMALL HUMPS OR LUMPS, THE FIRST BEING THE MOST PROMINENT
RELATIVELY SMALL MOUTH FOR A GREAT WHALE

---

rostrum

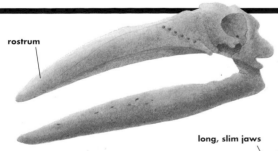

GRAY WHALE SKULL *(ABOVE)*
The main part of the gray whale's skull, containing the brain, is dwarfed by the enormous projecting jaws, which form the beaklike snout or rostrum.

HUMPBACK WHALE SKULL *(BELOW)*
Rorquals, such as the humpback whale, feed near the surface; they have longer, slimmer jaws and finer baleen than grays.

long, slim jaws

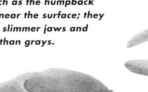

arched upper jaw

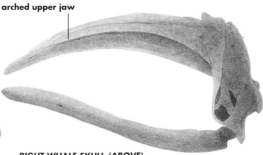

RIGHT WHALE SKULL *(ABOVE)*
The right whales, especially the bowhead, have a very arched upper jaw. From the middle of this hangs the longest and silkiest baleen of all the great whales.

Main illustrations Steve Kingston

COASTAL CRUISERS

ALTHOUGH MUCH REMAINS TO BE LEARNED ABOUT THE GRAY, IT HAS GIVEN US PLENTY OF OPPORTUNITIES TO STUDY IT, AS IT CLEARLY ENJOYS MEANDERING LAZILY ALONG IN SHALLOW COASTAL WATERS

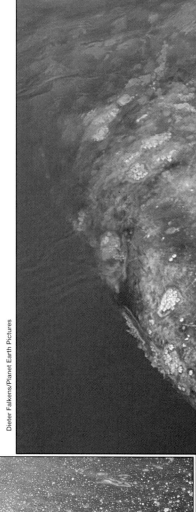

The gray whales' lives are dominated by their long migration. For up to four months of the year they are on the move, cruising steadily north in spring and then south in autumn, with hardly a pause for feeding or social interaction. In the Arctic they spend the summer feeding almost continually.

During the winter months, following the autumn southward migration, the mature California gray females give birth and feed their babies in the warm lagoons of Baja California in Mexico. During this time the males and younger adults mill around in deeper water, indulging in sexual play, rolling and resting, and generally loitering around. They may rest and sunbathe for up to half an hour at the surface, or on hotter days lie on the cooler seabed for up to ten minutes before rising to breathe.

SLOW AND STEADY

The gray idles along at 2.5–3.1 mph (4–5 km/h), cruises at about 6.2 mph (10 km/h) on migration, and can sprint at 12.5 mph (20 km/h) if alarmed; its breathing and submerging pattern remain fairly constant. It blows a jet of hot vapor about three or four times in one minute, then dives for three or four minutes, usually to depths of less than 164 ft (50 m).

If it intends to go deeper, perhaps to reach a rich food supply more than 330 ft (100 m) down, the gray blows and inhales up to six times in a minute or so, and then dives for up to ten minutes. It may resurface over 1,640 ft (500 m) from the point at which it submerged. Almost always, on the final blow as the whale dives, its tail flukes appear above the surface.

In general, gray whales prefer water less than 330 ft (100 m) deep and stay within a couple of miles of the shore. For such huge animals, they may swim alarmingly close to the beach—often to avoid killer whales, which rarely stray into coastal shallows. Grays have been seen rolling around in the surf, and

there are reports of partial strandings at low tide in only three feet (one meter) of water. But the whale merely waits for the next tide and floats itself off again, seemingly without ill effect. No other baleen whale can approach this type of inshore behavior. But life was not always easy for the gray whale. Being a fairly slow swimmer, and with its coast-hugging habits, the gray was an easy target for whalers, who rapidly reduced its populations to critically low levels, especially in the west Pacific.

IDENTIFYING FEATURES

Gray whales have many distinctive actions. One is spy-hopping, sometimes called pitchpoling or the lookout position. The whale turns itself head up and tail down, rears its head above the water as far as

The gray exhales via its twin nostrils, although the blow often merges into a single fountain (above).

Dieter Falkens/Planet Earth Pictures

Richard Coombes/Planet Earth Pictures

NAMING THE GRAY

The gray whale has been through a variety of official scientific names since it was first noticed and described by experts.

In 1777, German biologist Johann Erxleben christened it *Balaena gibbosa*—"humped baleen whale"—referring to the bowed body shape and the lumps on the back. In 1868, fossil-hunter Edward Cope called it *Rhachianectes glaucus*, or "gray swimmer along the rocky shore." In 1951, the gray was given its own family, Eschrichtiidae, in recognition of its distinctive features.

It was finally discovered that the species named from Atlantic fossils matched the live creatures in the west Pacific, so the experts, following scientific convention, went back to the original name *Eschrichtius robustus*, being the first scientific name given to the fossils. The genus and family names are in honor of Daniel Eschricht, professor of zoology in Copenhagen, who died in 1863.

The gray has many other local names along its range. Old-time whalers called it the mussel-digger, from its bed-feeding habits, and the scrag whale, due to its untidy appearance.

its flippers while thrashing the tail gently, then sinks slowly straight back into the water. Gray whales spy-hop regularly when on migration. They may be using their eyes to look for other whales, for enemies, or for cliffs and other landmarks on the nearby coastline.

The blow of the gray whale helps to distinguish it from other large whales in the area, such as the sperm whale. This was especially important in the days of whaling. The gray's blow is typically strong and vertical; it can be 10–13 ft (3–4 m) high. It is also characteristically loud, and in calm conditions it can be heard from well over half a mile (over one kilometer) away.

The blow contains a fountain of seawater that has leaked in through the mainly closed blowhole during the dive, along with warm, humid, stale air from the lungs, which condenses into steamy water vapor as it meets the colder outer air—like human breath on a winter's day—plus an aerosol of mucus and fluids from the linings of the air passages in the nose, windpipe, and lungs. ∎

The fibrous baleen plates can be clearly seen on this frolicking adult.

HABITATS

The gray whale spends its time in two very different ocean habitats. In the far north, in the Bering, Chukchi, and Okhotsk Seas, the water temperature is only a few degrees above freezing. Violent winter storms lash the area, the waves can be mountainous, and in autumn the sea freezes over as the pack ice spreads southward at walking pace. The grays approach the edge of the ice and may even dive under it to feed. Sometimes they get stuck under a large ice shelf, where, like any mammal, they may eventually drown. Wherever they are, grays tend to stay close to the coast or over mudbanks or sandbanks, in water that is usually less than 330 ft (100 m) deep. But the whales are well insulated by their under-skin layer of fatty blubber, 8 in (20 cm) or more in thickness. The blubber soon builds up in late spring as they start to feed, after migrating north in a relatively thin, blubberless condition.

Why do the whales brave such conditions? The cloudy water is a rich soup of nutrients stirred up from the bed and brought in by currents. In summer, the long hours of daylight are used by plant plankton to grow and thrive at an incredible rate. The plant plankton feeds tiny animals, and so forms the basis of the ocean food chains. These build up to feed giants like the gray and other whales.

WARM BUT HUNGRY

After the autumn journey south, the grays find themselves in a very different habitat. The breeding lagoons off Baja California are often still and calm, the water is clear, and its temperature is 68°F (20°C) or higher. These are much easier living conditions than in the Arctic. The grays lie on the sandy bottom and indulge in some courting and sexual activity, while the pregnant females give birth and

AMAZING FACTS

GRAYS IN THE NEWS

In a famous news story of 1988, two gray whales were discovered trapped near a small hole in the ice off Alaska. They had been marooned by the advancing ice, and the edge of the ice shelf was too far for them to locate. Plans were made to cut stepping-stone breathing holes in the ice, so that the whales could swim and surface their way along them, and so make their way to freedom.

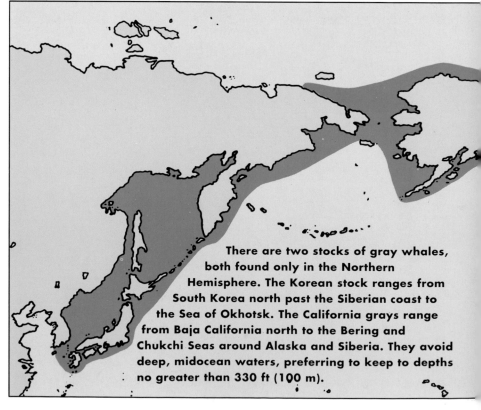

There are two stocks of gray whales, both found only in the Northern Hemisphere. The Korean stock ranges from South Korea north past the Siberian coast to the Sea of Okhotsk. The California grays range from Baja California north to the Bering and Chukchi Seas around Alaska and Siberia. They avoid deep, midocean waters, preferring to keep to depths no greater than 330 ft (100 m).

A calf frolics in the warm shallows off Mexico (left). *Soon it must join the pod on the long journey north.*

A gray rises to blow in British Columbia, Canada (above), *on the northern leg of its yearly migration.*

DISTRIBUTION

KEY

GRAY WHALE

feed their calves. The conditions are ideal for giving birth to babies, which have little insulating blubber and so would soon die in a colder environment.

But food presents a problem: The water is not rich in nutrients and supports less in the way of plankton than the cold northern seas, so the stay must be limited. Food stores laid down as blubber and body fat are used up, and a typical gray whale may lose about one-third of its body weight during this winter season. By the time spring approaches, the grays are hungry and ready to swim north, back to the rich Arctic and sub-Arctic feeding grounds. So it seems that the drastic change of habitats is a compromise to achieve good feeding and safe breeding. Only an animal as large as a whale could swim the distances involved and lay down the quantities of fat required for food reserves.

In recent years, there have been sightings of gray whales outside the usual seasonal range. Wanderers have been sighted off the coasts of Washington, British Columbia, Oregon, and northern California. This means some gray whales do not travel the full migratory journey north, but spend warmer months in these areas. This may be a consequence of the slowly increasing numbers following full protection of the species in 1946.

KILLERS

Large sharks, such as the great white, are occasional predators, picking on young or injured gray whales. But in both of its habitats, and on migration, the gray's only major predator is the orca or killer whale. Experiments have shown that gray whales swim rapidly away from taped sounds of killer whales. In the south, pods of killers attack mothers with calves. They bite at their lips, tongues, flukes, and other exposed, fleshy parts to cause wounds and bleeding. In defense, adult grays may place themselves between the killers and a calf, or a threatened gray may head for shallow water and kelp beds, where killer whales do not like to venture. Indeed, gray whales can navigate their way in water less than 33 ft (10 m) deep, even among the crashing surf. This familiarity with the shallows means that, compared to other inshore whales, grays rarely strand. If one is beached and dies, it is likely to be very old or sick or heavily parasitized.

DEVILFISH

Gray whales are also called devilfish and are given local names with a similar meaning in various languages, such as Japanese: *koku kujira*. This is partly because they are large, dark, and fishlike. But during the days of whaling, the grays also had a reputation for being fierce and ready to fight back if harpooned or rammed.

This was especially true when the breeding areas of Baja California were discovered in the 1850s. Whalers began to take what they thought might be easy catches, in the sheltered waters. But the

Richard Coombes/Planet Earth Pictures

BAJA CALIFORNIA

The warm, subtropical lagoons lying along the coasts of the Baja California peninsula in Mexico are ideal calving areas for the whales, which swim down to the region for the winter. The bays and inlets are calm and sheltered, although the waters are not particularly rich in nutrients. The surrounding scrubland is very desertlike, so there is little runoff from the land and hardly any rivers to wash nutrients into the sea. The coastline is almost free of human settlement, except where whale-watching businesses have grown up in recent years. The whales' main breeding sites are Laguna Ojo de Liebre, Laguna San Ignacio, Laguna Guerro Negro, and Estero Soledad.

The only sizable town in the area is La Paz, the capital of the Mexican state of Baja California Sur. Situated on the southeastern tip of the peninsula, it has about 140,000 inhabitants; the whole state has a population of fewer than 350,000 people.

TEMPERATURE

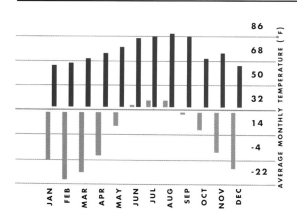

- THE ARCTIC
- BAJA CALIFORNIA

Temperatures are given for both extremes of the gray's migration route. It is only in the summer that Arctic temperatures rise above freezing, while the winter quarters in Baja California are warm all year round.

mother gray whales fought back to protect themselves and their calves. One whaling expedition in Magdalena Bay, in 1856, recorded three men badly injured, another six shocked, two boats sunk, and most of the others damaged from ramming. And this was before one whale had been caught.

Gray whales have been observed reacting violently to aircraft and ship noises, and they have even tried to pursue low-flying aircraft. Yet this is in great contrast to their peaceful and tolerant nature in modern whale-watching situations. ∎

NEIGHBORS

The subtropical waters of the Pacific lagoons are poorer in nutrients than the High Arctic waters, but many animals come to enjoy the warmth, breeding alongside the whales in the sheltered bays.

HORNED PUFFIN

Puffins exploit the mud and prey animals disturbed by the gray whale as it plows along the seabed.

PACIFIC WALRUS

Walruses grub in the seabed for food. They eat bivalve shellfish, such as clams and scallops.

Neighbor and enemy illustrations Peter Bull

USA

MEXICO

BAJA
CALIFORNIA

LA PAZ

Pacific Ocean

BAJA CALIFORNIA

Baja California is a 800-mile (1,280-km) strip of mountainous, arid land on the Pacific coast of North America, running south from the California-Mexico border. La Paz, on the southern tip, lies near the tropic of Cancer (23°27' north of the equator). Between Baja and the mainland lies the Gulf of California.

KILLER WHALE
Killers hunt in packs, using sound signals to coordinate an attack on their toothless cousins, the gray whales.

LEATHERBACK

Largest of all sea turtles, the leatherback lives in warm waters off North and South American coasts.

SEA OTTERS

These large otters live in coastal colonies, where they dive for shellfish. They rarely come ashore.

ARCTIC TERN

This is one of the few animals that has a longer migration route than the gray whale.

STELLER'S SEA LION

These seals live around the rim of the North Pacific, from the Sea of Japan to San Miguel, California.

ELEPHANT SEAL

Elephant seals sometimes mingle with pods of gray whales. The huge males weigh over two tons.

SOCIAL STRUCTURE

The gray whale is one of the less social of the whales; it does not seem to form permanent groupings or male-female bonds, as in some other whale species. The only strong and enduring association is that between a mother and her calf, a relationship that lasts about one year.

Gray whales usually swim on their own, or with one or two others, but they do not interact closely. As many as fifteen individuals may swim close to each other on migration, but this is still a loose association. At the summer feeding grounds, grays form large mixed schools, but this is mainly for the reason of gathering at the same food source. In fact, if gray whales are found together, it is usually for the reasons of feeding, breeding, or migrating.

In the winter breeding grounds, the grays segregate by age and sex. In the sheltered bays and inlets are females with their calves, while outside the main lagoons males and young adults gather and may indulge in courting. Sexual behavior has been observed at all times of the year, at all points along the length of the migration route, but actual mating groups of up to eight animals tend to occur most frequently in November and December.

SOUNDS AND SONGS

Many whales, especially the humpback, are famed for their songs. The eerie sounds include wails, grunts, and clicks, and they echo for many miles through the oceans. For years, scientists were

Gray whales sport in lively fashion during their winter stay in the southern lagoons (right).

unsure whether gray whales sang. This is partly because they were difficult to track and record on migration, but also because the lagoons around Baja California are noisy with the sounds of pistol shrimp and other background activity.

The gray whale has now been recorded, and is known to make several sounds. There are grunts, pulses, clicks, clacks, beeps, moans, and knocks. The gray may blow out air in a characteristic bubble blast with a frequency of 130–840 Hz (Hz, or Hertz, represent cycles per second), or it may make a subsurface bubble trail at 250–850 Hz; both of these noises last about three seconds and can be heard just over a mile (over two kilometers) away. There are also very high whines at the upper extreme of our own hearing limit, 20,000 Hz. Calves attract their mothers with a low resonating pulse, like a buzzing hum.

In general, however, the sounds made by gray whales do not appear to have the social significance and communication aspects that are found in the humpback, for example, or in toothed whales, such as dolphins and killer whales.

GIGI THE SINGING GRAY

Some sounds were recorded from the only large whale to be held in captivity, the young female gray known to her keepers as Gigi. In 1971, with

WINTER FUN

Normally unsociable, grays are a little more friendly in winter when they gather to breed. The Mexican lagoons resound with tail-slapping and blowing adults (below).

Illustration Robin Carter/Wildlife Art Agency

François Gohier/Ardea

in SIGHT

HELPING OUT

In some animals, members of a species will help others of their group or species when in danger. This is seen clearly in social insects such as ants and bees, when a worker will sting an intruder and sacrifice its life for the good of the hive.

Biologists refer to this type of action as altruistic behavior. If the helped animal is a close relative of the helper, then the helper's actions can be interpreted as giving the genes that they share (through being related) a better chance of survival.

Gray whales, like several other whale species, have been known to exhibit helpful behavior. An injured female may be supported by several males so that she can conserve energy and reach the surface to breathe. The males may also protect her from killer whales. Breeding, too, may involve a third whale, which supports the mating pair. Females, however, do not seem to go to the aid of a male in difficulty, but any nearby adult—of either sex—may move in to protect a calf from killer whales.

permission from the International Whaling Commission (IWC), she was taken into captivity from Laguna Ojo de Liebre, Baja California, to the Sea World Oceanarium in San Diego. The aims were to study her behavior and also the feasibility of captive breeding. The whale used was actually Gigi II; the original Gigi, another young female, was caught the previous year but did not survive the transfer.

When Gigi arrived in her enormous transport tank, she was over 2 tons in weight and 19 ft (5.8 m)

WHAT'S UP?

Spy-hopping (left) *is a favorite activity of the grays; rearing up enables them to see their surroundings.*

long. After a year of eating about 1,980 lb (900 kg) of squid each day, she had grown almost 6.5 ft (2 m) in length and close to 4.5 tons in weight. Gigi was released back into the wild and tracked by her radio transmitter for several weeks, and then was sighted some time later, still alive and well. She provided scientists with many insights into the feeding behavior of gray whales, as well as swimming methods and sound production—but, unfortunately, no information on social interactions. ∎

MIGRATION

The California grays spend the summer in the Bering Sea. They feed in mixed herds near St. Lawrence Island, and some pass through the Bering Straits into the Chukchi Sea. They leave the Arctic in October, spending all of November on the move, and the main groups reach Baja California in early December. The females come close to the shore, to the sheltered lagoons, to calve at the end of January. After the warm winter rest, the gray whales prepare to set off north again in early March. The males, females, and calves join up for the return journey, reaching the Arctic region around the middle to the end of May.

ON THE MOVE

Gray whales cruise at a steady 4–6 mph (7–10 km/h) while migrating, depending on the conditions. How do they find their way? They may simply stay in shallow water to hug the coastline. Also, they regularly spy-hop, perhaps to spot landmarks or just to keep land in view. For the southward migration, the

THE JOURNEY SOUTH

Pregnant females lead the way (below), *followed by adult males, juveniles, and mothers with calves.*

Jeff Foott/Survival Anglia

heavily pregnant females leave the Arctic first, swimming straight and fast in ones and twos. They are followed by females who have just weaned their calves and others who are soon to be, or may already be, pregnant. Then the procession slows down and larger, looser groups of immature females and males, plus adult males, follow.

In both directions, the early days of migration see the whales traveling singly or in small groups, rarely of more than five or six. Later they team up in twos or sometimes threes, and later still in loose groups of ten or more. This may give them some protection—against sharks in the warmer southern waters, or against killer whales as they head north. The grays rarely stop to feed on the main leg of the migration, and by the time they arrive at the destination, they may have lost up to one-third of their body weight. Not all of the California gray whales make the whole journey to the Arctic, however; some stay off British Columbia to feed. These are a mixed bunch including both sexes and all ages.

THE KOREAN GRAYS

On the other side of the Pacific, the Korean stock of gray whales makes a similar north-south migration. However, these whales are very rare, and their

The epic migration takes a heavy toll on the gray whale's fat and energy reserves (left).

François Gohier/Ardea

A calf cruises close to its mother (above). *Newborns have very little blubber and must grow rapidly in order to cope with the cold waters up north.*

movements are known with far less detail. It is thought that they go north in spring, beginning in about March. By May they reach the Sea of Okhotsk off the south Siberian coast for the summer feed. They begin their return in October and arrive back in the area of Korea in late November. These grays may rest and give birth among the inlets and islands of Korea's southern coast, or perhaps around the south of Japan's Kyushu Island. ∎

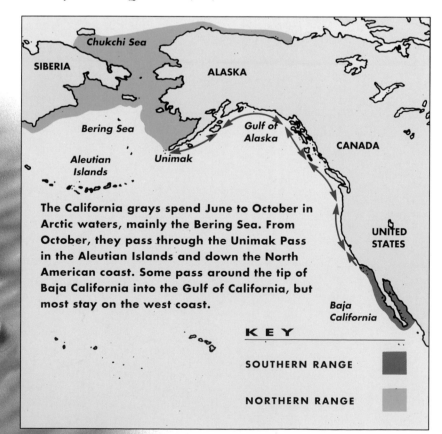

The California grays spend June to October in Arctic waters, mainly the Bering Sea. From October, they pass through the Unimak Pass in the Aleutian Islands and down the North American coast. Some pass around the tip of Baja California into the Gulf of California, but most stay on the west coast.

KEY

SOUTHERN RANGE

NORTHERN RANGE

Illustration Mark Stewart/Wildlife Art Agency

KEY FACTS

● Migrating south after the summer feed, grays cover about 100–125 miles (160–200 km) per day. Migrating north again, however, after the winter rest and breeding, they cover only 50 miles (80 km) per day. They move more slowly northward for various reasons: There are mothers with young calves, opposing ocean currents, and their bodies are in poorer condition after the winter rest and fast.

● The California grays are credited with making the longest migrations of any mammal—perhaps over 12,000 miles (20,000 km) each year—although recent research suggests that some humpback whales of the southeast Pacific may equal or even exceed this journey. In an average gray whale's lifetime of forty years, this distance is equivalent to swimming to the moon and back.

FOOD AND FEEDING

Gray whales feed up in northern waters between June and October. The food must last them for the migration south, the winter rest, and the return journey north. Little wonder that, at the height of summer, an adult gray whale consumes well over a ton of food each day. When it returns next spring, it may be only two-thirds of its autumn weight.

FEEDING HABITS

Gray whales usually feed in water less than 330 ft (100 m) deep, and often only 165 ft (50 m); rarely do they dive to more than 400 ft (120 m). At a rich site, more than 100 individuals may gather in a loose group. The grays eat small crustaceans, such as isopods and amphipods; these resemble small shrimp and are related to the beach fleas seen hopping on shore. A gray whale will also swallow other mud-dwelling animals, such as worms, shrimp, and mollusks.

Grays feed by plowing along the seabed. They take in the top few layers of sediment, or stir it up, then use their baleen to filter animals from it. Other baleen whales feed by gulping in huge mouthfuls of water or skimming through water that contains small swimming animals. The gray usually dives to the seabed and turns on to its side—usually to its right. As a result, the baleen on this side becomes worn.

A gray may filter and swallow as it goes, trailing a plume of mud from the mouth and leaving a furrow behind it in the seabed, or it may make two

passes. The first stirs up the mud and the second gathers the disturbed creatures, after the heavier mud and gravel has settled back to the bottom. The whale may make several such furrows before surfacing. If it has not already swallowed, it may force the mud through the baleen as it surfaces, using the pumping action of the tongue, which at well over a

in SIGHT

A WORM'S WORK

Gray whales are thought to contribute to the health and productivity of the ocean floor by their plowing activities, similar to huge versions of earthworms on land. They prevent the mud from settling and hardening, which would exclude air and so lower the amount of life in it. A gray whale can leave an oval furrow in the sand up to 33 ft (10 m) long, 23 ft (7 m) wide, and 16 in (40 cm) deep; or separate pits 8 ft (2.5 m) long, 5 ft (1.5 m) wide, and 4 in (10 cm) deep. The young of its prey animals are so small that they pass through the baleen sieve and fall back to the seabed, to recolonize the area. Walruses, which also gouge up the seafloor, help contribute to its tilling.

Illustration Chris Turnbull/Wildlife Art Agency

PLOWING A FURROW

The whale plows its head through the mud or sand, mouth open, and retracts its tongue to suck in the mud, or scoops up the sediment and any creatures in it. The mud is then filtered out the other side of the mouth, leaving the animals trapped on the inside of the baleen.

After feeding, the gray whale surfaces to refill its lungs. Then, with a mighty thrust of the tail flukes (right), down it dives again.

Hanne and Jens Erikson/Aquila

ton in weight has plenty of muscle power. The trapped creatures are licked off and swallowed from inside the baleen curtain. The whale then blows several times to refresh the air in its lungs and dives again.

The gray's baleen plates are stiff, stout, and short for filtering coarse material. About 160 plates hang from the upper jaws; each is 16–20 in (40–50 cm) long and about 10 in (25 cm) wide. It is grayish white and has around 40 yellowish fringing bristles or fibers.

SNACKS EN ROUTE

Gray whales occasionally gulp-feed in midwater, in the manner of other baleen whales. During migration, they may skim-feed like right whales. Their stomach contents have included small fish, such as herring, anchovy, and smelt, and squid and shrimp. Grays have been seen to swim around a school of fish to herd them together, and then swim up vertically from below, gulping as they go, in the manner of humpback and other rorqual whales. ■

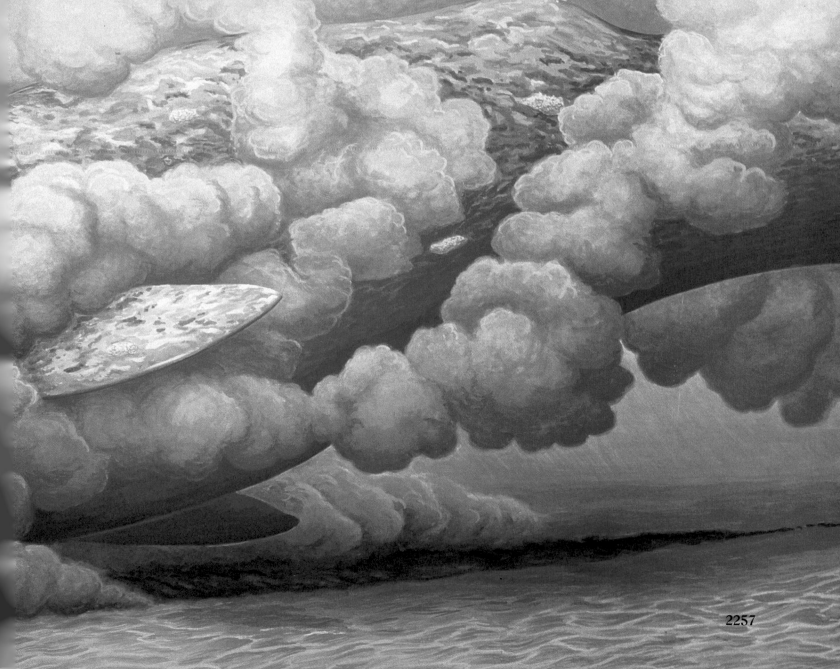

REPRODUCTION

During the summer feeding frenzy, gray whales are usually too busy to indulge in courtship or sexual behavior, but as they migrate south, their intentions turn to reproduction. Males and females swim close and may caress each other with their flukes or flippers. As they approach the winter areas, groups of males and females loll about, but there are no strong pair bonds: Males leave and join other groups at random, and females mate several times with several males in the group.

The males are not aggressive with each other, as in some whale species, and there is no fighting or overt competition. Males seem to rely on sperm competition—producing enough sperm to displace any that the female may already have received. The male gray whale has large testicles and a penis over 3.3 ft (1 m) long to achieve this.

ASSISTED MATING

Mating has been observed at all times of the year, but it becomes more common toward the end of the autumn migration. The peak time for conception for California gray whales is during early December. Only females who gave birth the previous year, and whose calves are now growing up, are usually receptive to males; those about to give birth or with newborn calves are usually not.

FROM BIRTH TO DEATH

GESTATION: 12 MONTHS (MAY BE EXTENDED IN SOME CONDITIONS TO 14)
NUMBER OF BABIES: 1; TWINS ARE RARE
SIZE AT BIRTH: 15–16.5 FT (4.5–5 M) LONG,
WEIGHT AT BIRTH: 1,100–2,650 LB (500–1,200 KG)
SUCKLING PERIOD: USUALLY 7–8 MONTHS, MAXIMUM 10 MONTHS
LENGTH AT SEXUAL MATURITY: MALE 36.5 FT (11.1 M), FEMALE 38.4 FT (11.7 M) ON AVERAGE
AGE AT SEXUAL MATURITY: 5–11 YEARS, AVERAGE 8 YEARS
SIZE AND AGE AT PHYSICAL MATURITY: 42.6 FT (13 M) FOR MALES, 46 FT (14 M) FOR FEMALES, AGE 35–40 YEARS
AVERAGE LIFESPAN: 40 YEARS OR MORE. MAXIMUM RECORDED LIFESPAN 77 YEARS

Illustration Kim Thompson

Mating may involve two, three, or as many as five animals; the extras may help the mating pair to stay afloat. Actual copulation lasts 30–100 seconds; the pair involved may lie on their sides at the surface for up to an hour and copulate several times, waving their topside flippers in the air. Another one or two males may position themselves on the far side of the female, often in the vertical spy-hop position, to support her during this time.

BIRTH DAYS

Most of the gray whale calves are born in Baja California's Laguna Ojo de Liebre, Laguna San Ignacio, Laguna Guerro Negro, and Estero Soledad. The majority arrive within one month of each other, with the peak in mid-January. The actual birth is in water only 33 ft (10 m) deep, and the calf emerges tail first, as in many other whales.

The new calf often has difficulty swimming and coordinating its movements to surface and breathe or to suckle its mother's milk from the teats on her rear underside. The mother is attentive and highly protective, however, and helps by holding it at the surface with her back or flipper. In the shallow lagoons, mother and calf stay close and touch often. The youngster has barely any blubber at this stage, but the water is warm and insulation is hardly necessary.

By the time that the northward migration looms, the calf is about

MOTHER'S HELP
The newborn calf needs encouragement to take its first breath, so its mother gently nudges it to the surface (below).

OUT OF ACTION

PESTS AND DISEASES

Gray whales succumb to killer whales, and rarely to large sharks. Otherwise, they have no natural predators. However, like other baleen whales, they may suffer from a variety of diseases such as cancer, stomach ulcers, heart disease, pneumonia, jaundice, and osteoarthritis. They also have internal parasites such as worms, which may take more of a toll as the whale gets older. The gray whale also has the most external pests of any whale: These include whale lice, which are about the size of a large coin.

two months old. When it reaches the Arctic it will have built up a thick underlayer of blubber, made from the nutrients in the milk of the mother. The calf is also bolder and leaps and breaches some distance from its mother. She has not eaten for perhaps eight months, so she feeds hungrily to restore her body fat and keep up the milk supplies. At the end of the summer, the calf is usually weaned, but the mother still protects it on the way, until they reach the warm lagoons again.

THE REPRODUCTIVE CYCLE

The average gray whale female gives birth every other year. Her usual cycle is a gestation period of twelve to thirteen months, followed by seven or eight months of lactation, and then three or four months of rest and recuperation. There are, however, occasional sightings of a possibly pregnant female with a calf still feeding on her milk.

The gray calf grows at an incredible rate, putting on over 2 lb (1 kg) every hour through the summer. Most young reach sexual maturity at about eight years old, when the male is 36.5 ft (11.1 m) long and the female 38.4 ft (11.7 m). The female usually remains slightly larger than the male throughout life, and full physical maturity is not attained until after thirty years. Much of this information about the whales' age comes from the waxy earplugs that fill the outer ear canals of baleen whales. These plugs usually add on a layer each year, much like the growth rings in a tree trunk, so zoologists can analyze the plugs to check a whale's age. In a large adult gray whale, the earplug can be over 16 in (40 cm) long. ∎

Adult grays pass their warm, balmy days down south, frolicking and mating (right).

WHALERS AND WATCHERS

THE GRAY'S SLOW COASTAL MIGRATIONS ONCE MADE IT A SITTING DUCK FOR HARPOONERS—BUT THEY ALSO EXPOSED IT TO WHALE-WATCHERS, AND TODAY IT IS WATCHED BY TOURISTS IN DINGHIES

The inshore habits and slow swimming of the gray whale made it an easy target for the early shore-based whalers. After centuries of small-scale hunting by native people, there followed the boom years of commercial whaling, which led the whale to the edge of extinction. The gray, however, has had a reprieve: Although the Korean stock remains rare, the California stock goes vigorously forward.

But the future was once far less rosy for the gray; its small populations in the Atlantic, for example, succumbed to the impact of whaling. In fact, it may never have been common in the North Atlantic. Perhaps its disappearance, by the early 18th century, was hastened by whaling, but not due solely to it.

GRAYS IN THE EASTERN PACIFIC

From ancient times until 1840, there were perhaps 30,000 California gray whales. Before the mid-19th century, grays had been hunted in small numbers by native peoples along their migration route and in the Arctic. These people included Aleuts, American and Asian Inuits, and various American Indians, who rowed after them in canoes in the Bay of Vancouver and among the Queen Charlotte Islands. The grays were taken for their rich meat, oil, baleen, and hides. In Baja California, however, the grays were almost entirely undisturbed, since hardly anyone lived along the arid coasts.

COMMERCIAL WHALING

Large-scale hunting of the California grays began in Magdalena Bay in 1845 and finished with full species protection in 1946. At the lowest ebb, the eastern Pacific population was said to be no more than 200–300 animals, although recent analysis has cast doubt on this figure. Given the gray's normal breeding rate, it is hard to understand how it could have recovered to 20,000 or more animals today.

By the 1850s, New England whalers began to scour the region for gray whales, having hunted out their more traditional areas around the western North Atlantic. The whalers followed the migration routes south and found the calving lagoons. Then came the main killing years of 1855–65. Shore-based whalers took their two chances each year to attack the passing whales; they fished for the rest of the year to boost their income. By 1875, some 11,000 grays had been killed in the calving areas and along the southern parts of the migration route, and the large groups of migrating whales were reduced to tens and fifties.

The dangers of extermination for the gray whale were recognized as early as the 1870s. Some New England whaling captains warned that the grays

D. Gotshall/Planet Earth Pictures

This young gray whale died after its flukes became entangled in a loose section of gill net (above).

Dieter Falkens/Planet Earth Pictures

THEN & NOW

This map shows the former and current distribution of the gray whale.

 FORMER   **CURRENT**

There are no gray whales in the North Atlantic, but they certainly existed there in days gone by. In the early 1600s, a sketch from Iceland portrayed what is probably a gray whale. In 1725, anecdotes of the Royal Society of London described how whalers of eastern North America hunted the "scrag whale"—a local name for the gray. The whalers' activities combined with the gray's natural rarity to push it into extinction.

were in danger, and, therefore, so was the livelihood of the whalers. In his 1874 book *The Marine Mammals of the Northwestern Coast of North America*, ex-whaler Captain Charles Scammon said that grays could disappear forever.

SAVED BY THE CRUDE

Boat-based whaling for grays along the Pacific coast of North America declined from the mid-1870s; shore-based whaling continued until about 1900, then faded. This was partly due to the increasing rarity of the gray whale, but also due to the rise of the petroleum industry. The more easily obtained oils and fuels from the crude of Texan wells took the place of whale oil. In any case, during the boom years of oceangoing whalers and factory ships, the

Although watching is much better than hunting, it can unsettle the whales in their breeding lagoons.

ALONGSIDE MAN

A SECOND-BEST WHALE

In the main years of commercial whaling—for the grays, the third quarter of the last century—almost every part of the carcass could be used. The muscle was meat for both human and animal consumption. The blubbery oil and fat were used as fuel—in lamps and for heating, cooking, and fires. The skin was preserved and used as leather for footwear, cloaks, and tents. The baleen was used much as we use plastics now: It was cut, carved, bent, and fashioned into needles, cooking items, tools, garment stays, and many other objects. It was also carved and sculpted into brooches, reliefs, and pendants. However, the grays were not the ideal whales to hunt and use; this dubious honor belonged to the right whales. In the grays' winter breeding lagoons, the mothers fought gamely against the whalers to protect their calves. The gray's baleen was difficult to work, and the oil and fat yields from wintering gray whales were also low, since the whales did not need thick blubber in the warmer waters.

grays were never a main target. Most of the slaughter took place far to the south and centered on blues, humpbacks, and other rorquals in the Antarctic Ocean. Whaling for grays started again in about 1913. The whale gained partial protection in 1936, but hunting continued sporadically until it received full protection from the International Whaling Commission, (IWC) in 1946. Its numbers have risen steadily since 1937.

In the 1960s, some Mexican groups suggested that controlled numbers of gray whales could be caught and canned for the pet food industry. But most people have come to realize that the gray whales in the area are worth much more alive than dead, as the basis of the whale-watching business around Baja California.

THE KOREAN STOCK

The history of the Korean stock in the west Pacific is much less clear. Whaling around Japan has been recorded from the 10th century; there were sightings of grays migrating along the west coasts of the Japanese islands of Honshu and more northerly Hokkaido. Another group may have migrated east to the southern Japanese island of Kyushu. The Seto Inland Sea was a possible calving ground, along with the bays and inlets of southern Korea.

Through the 1700s and 1800s, probably fifty grays were killed per year, and the species has been almost unknown in some southern parts of its range since the 1890s. Possibly the increase in boat traffic drove them from the Seto Sea. The original population of the Korean stock was probably never very high, perhaps as few as 2,000 or as many as 10,000.

In an odd reversal of fortune, gray whales trapped in the ice receive help from Native North Americans. In days gone by, the people would probably have killed them for meat and oil.

In the summer feeding grounds, commercial whaling from the turn of this century to the 1930s was very damaging. This followed catches in the mid-19th century in the Sea of Okhotsk, where records and weighings show low amounts of blubber and meat from each carcass, indicating that young grays were the main targets. There were about 1,500 recorded kills by shore-based whalers in Korean waters from 1910 to 1933, but many other catches may have gone unrecorded. From 1910, there were perhaps 2,000 commercial kills in the west Pacific.

Since the grays received full protection in 1946, small catches have been allowed for traditional reasons. Along the Asian coasts, some of these catches have been taken by large commercial factory ships, and then supposedly handed over to the native peoples concerned. Some observers say, however, that parts of gray whale carcasses found their way to the local mink farms to support the fur industry.

STILL RARE

Today, there are perhaps only 200–300 gray whales in the Korean stock. Political factors in the area have been one barrier to accurate figures; as with the Atlantic grays in former times, it has been suggested that the west Pacific sightings are vagrants from the California stock, but numbers in the Sea of Okhotsk and around Kamchatka in the spring make this unlikely. The two stocks of gray whales, California and Korean, are geographically isolated, and their migration routes are probably at least partly learned. So the possibility of transplanting a group across the Pacific, with successful migration and breeding, would require research and careful planning. ■

François Gohier/Ardea

INTO THE FUTURE

While large wild species in almost every other part of the world are suffering critical population declines, surveys suggest that the numbers of California gray whales are actually rising at the rate of about 3 percent per year. In the early 1990s, there was no indication that this rate of increase was slowing down, or that the numbers of whales were leveling off. Such a leveling-off usually occurs when a population reaches the carrying capacity of the environment—the number of creatures that the environment can support with available resources of food, space, shelter or homes, and other factors.

This information indicates that the lower population estimate for prewhaling times, of 15,000 gray whales in the east Pacific, may well be too low. If the environment and resources today can support higher numbers, perhaps 25,000 or more, then they probably could a few centuries ago, too.

PREDICTION

A CAUSE FOR CAUTIOUS OPTIMISM
Numbers of California gray whales are rising, and there is every good reason to suppose that they will continue to do so—provided that their northern feeding grounds are not overfished. The Korean or west Pacific stock is extremely endangered, however, and will need close monitoring to control "traditional" culls.

There is no longer a danger to the gray whale from mass slaughter, but there may be other threats in the future. Unregulated tourism could disturb the mothers and calves in the breeding lagoons. Whale-watching takes place in some very remote places, and policing every expedition is impossible.

Water pollution is another pressing problem. It includes oil spills, as well as agricultural and manufacturing chemical runoff from the land. The 1989 *Exxon Valdez* tanker spillage in Alaska caused the death of countless seabirds and several killer whales; if such a disaster hit the gray whales' summer feeding grounds, devastating mortality could ensue.

Whales can easily become trapped in nets used for fishing, especially the immense, curtainlike gill nets draped into the sea that are intended for tuna and similar fish. During the 1980s about sixty gray whales were found tangled and drowned in this way—and by no means were all the gill nets examined for this particular problem. ■

WHALE-WATCHING

Much of the coastline of southern Baja California is too dry for agriculture, so the main industry is tourism. People come to the long, sandy beaches to swim; they also come to watch whales, especially in areas like Magdalena Bay, where visitors are almost guaranteed to see gray whales on any winter's day.

There are strict laws to protect the whales from intrusion, both in the wintering areas and along the migration routes. This is mainly to avoid disturbing the pregnant females or the mothers with their new calves. Boats are forbidden to approach too close to the whales. However, if a whale approaches the boat of its own accord, then this is acceptable, and very lucky for the occupants.

The whales may even spy-hop to look at the whale-watchers. The huge head rears 10 ft (3 m) vertically from the water, and the whale beats its tail to maintain its erect posture, causing powerful swirls and currents. It may also swivel to get an all-around view. The whales seem content to be stroked and patted; some individual whales regularly approach the boats. Even mothers with calves show little caution; a calf may prod and push an inflatable dingy like a giant blow-up toy, while some adults lift their snouts and lay them on low dinghies.

People also watch from the shore. Up to a million people gather on Point Loma, near San Diego Bay, each spring and autumn to watch the whales swim past only a couple of hundred yards from the shore. However, in recent years, some whales have taken to migrating up to 30 miles (50 km) out at sea; this may be connected with the increased inshore boat traffic.

Illustration Mike Dodd/Wildlife Art Agency

KILLER WHALES

RELATIONS

Killer whales and pilot whales belong to the suborder Odontoceti, or toothed whales. Other members of the suborder include:

RIVER DOLPHINS

DOLPHINS

PORPOISES

SPERM WHALE

BEAKED WHALES

ZEFA

ORDER

Cetacea
(whales)

SUPERFAMILY

Delphinoidea
(dolphins)

FAMILY

Globicephalidae
(killer and pilot whales [sometimes included in the main dolphin family Delphinidae])

(melon-headed whale [sometimes included in the Globicephalidae, sometimes in the dolphin family Delphinidae, or even in its own family Peponocephalidae])

CLEVER KILLERS

THEY CRUISE ANY OCEAN, FROM THE ICY POLES TO THE WARMEST TROPICS. THEY EAT ANY FOOD, FROM FISH AND SQUID TO GIANT WHALES. IN FACT, THEY DO PRETTY MUCH WHAT THEY WANT

Killer whales are big. An adult male can be over 26 ft (8 m) long and weigh well over six tons, as heavy as two zoo elephants. Killer whales are also curious; they often approach ships and divers and show little fear. They can also "stand" upright, half out of the water, to take a look around—a pose called spyhopping or pitchpoling. Killers live up to their name, too: They are among the fastest, most powerful hunters in the sea and can tackle almost any prey.

But they are also smart and cooperative. They use an amazing array of sound signals and visual signs to talk to each other as they hunt, rest, play, court, breed, and bring up their young.

There are three species of killer whales. The most familiar and common is called the killer whale, great killer whale, or orca; it is the largest of the three species. The other two species are the slightly smaller false killer whale and the much smaller pygmy, or dwarf, killer whale.

All three killers belong to the mammal group of the cetaceans—the whales, dolphins, and porpoises—which is split into two main subgroups. The Odontoceti, or toothed whales, includes dolphins, porpoises, narwhals, white whales, sperm whales, and beaked whales. The Mysticeti, or baleen whales, comprises such giants as the humpback, gray, fin, sei, right, and blue whales. The killers, with their mouthful of pointed teeth, are three of the 66-odd species of odontocetes. They have similarities with the true dolphins, so they are classified with them in the superfamily Delphinoidea.

DEPENDING ON YOUR VIEWPOINT, THE GREAT KILLER WHALE IS EITHER THE LARGEST DOLPHIN OR A SMALL WHALE

Some experts regard the three killer whales as true dolphins, in the family Delphinidae, but the killers and dolphins differ in many ways. Killers are bigger, for a start. They lack the beak-shaped mouth and have fewer teeth; their neck vertebrae are different; they are all black and white; they have a comparatively tall dorsal fin and long flippers. Because of these differences, many experts now place the killer whales in their own family, the Globicephalidae: "globe-heads," or "round-heads."

A killer whale (right) *breaches, lifting its body almost clear of the water.*

Pygmy killer whales (above) *usually travel in pods, or families, of about ten animals.*

Another two species of whales also show many differences with dolphins but share common features with the killer whales. These are the long-finned pilot whale, or pothead whale, and the short-finned pilot whale, with their similarly bulbous foreheads, so they are usually included with the killer whales in the family Globicephalidae. At about 16–23 ft (5–7 m) long, the long-finned pilot whale is slightly larger than the short-finned, which measures 13–20 ft (4–6 m).

The pilot whales' name may come from their habit of swimming in single file, with the leading whale as the "pilot." This is the term used in the mariner's sense—the expert at guiding a vessel in and out of a harbor or other hazardous route. Another explanation is the belief that pilot whales once guided fishermen to schools of herring and other fish. (However, the sailors may have simply observed the whales going about their natural business of feeding, and, from this, they deduced the presence of a fish school.)

LONG AGO

All whales, dolphins, and porpoises seem to derive from a group of land-living carnivores called mesonychids (mess-o-NIE-kids), which lived 30–65 million years ago. These meat-eaters looked rather wolflike in earlier forms; some stayed on land and developed into horselike grazers, while others took to a new environment for mammals: the sea.

One of the oldest cetaceans was *Pakicetus*, which lived some 50 million years ago. It had only

The elusive melon-headed whales (above) *prefer the warmer waters of the world.*

D. McSweeney/ZEFA

David Fleetham/Natural Science Photos

2267

LONG-FINNED PILOT WHALE

Globicephala melaena
(globe-EE-seff-AH-la mell-EEN-a)

LONG-FINNED SUBSPECIES:
G. M. MELAENA
(NORTH ATLANTIC)
G. M. EDWARDI
(SOUTHERN HEMISPHERE)

THE KILLERS' FAMILY TREE

It is fairly certain that the three killer whale species are closely related to each other, and the two pilot whales to each other. But it is not possible to give a definitive family tree for how these five species are related to the melon-headed whale and to other dolphins; the truth is that we do not know. Several classification systems exist; the one shown here separates the killer, pilot, and melon-headed whales as the family Globicephalidae.

SHORT-FINNED PILOT WHALE

Globicephala macrorhynchus
(globe-EE-seff-AH-la mack-ro-RINK-uss)

MELON-HEADED WHALE

Peponocephala electra
(pep-O-no-seff-AH-la eh-LEK-tra)

The melon-headed whale is sometimes called the many-toothed blackfish, though of course it is not a fish but a mammal. In fact, in various places at various times, the name blackfish has been applied to each species of killer whale, and sometimes to the pilot whales, too. This is perhaps understandable: A quick glance at the dark form of a killer, pilot, or melon-headed whale from the surface would not reveal the white patches along the belly and underside.

All illustrations Richard Tibbitts

just taken to the water, and it looked like a large otter. Yet in a short time, in evolutionary terms, cetaceans had become much as we know them today. They lost almost all traces of fur, their forelimbs became flippers, and their rear limbs disappeared. The tails developed flukes, and their nostrils moved to the top of the skull to become the blowhole.

By about 30 million years ago, the earliest true toothed whales swam in the seas and had sharklike teeth. One was *Prosqualodon* (pro-SKWAH-lo-don), whose fossils have been uncovered in South America, Australia, and New Zealand. It lived about 30–25 million years ago.

In the Southern Hemisphere during the Miocene epoch, 25–5 million years ago, some squalodontids may have split from the main dolphin group to give rise to the ancestors of today's killer whales and possibly the pilot whales. Another evolutionary branch produced the more primitive beaked whales, freshwater dolphins, porpoises, and spiral-tusked narwhals. Today, the killer and pilot whales occupy almost all the world's oceans. ■

TOOTHED WHALES

DOLPHINS AND OTHER TOOTHED WHALES

FALSE KILLER WHALE
Pseudorca crassidens
(*sude-ORK-ah KRASS-ee-denz*)

This whale is known as far north as Norway in the Atlantic Ocean but prefers the warmer waters.

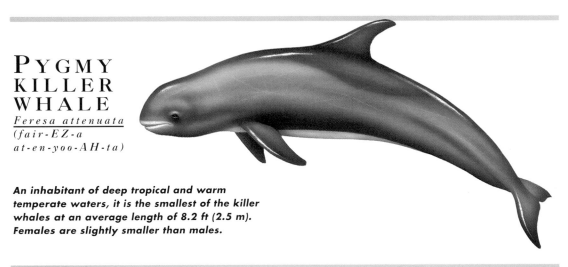

PYGMY KILLER WHALE
Feresa attenuata
(*fair-EZ-a at-en-yoo-AH-ta*)

An inhabitant of deep tropical and warm temperate waters, it is the smallest of the killer whales at an average length of 8.2 ft (2.5 m). Females are slightly smaller than males.

KILLER WHALE
Orcinus orca (*or-KEEN-us ORK-a*)

The largest and most common of the killer whales, this species is also known as the great killer whale, or orca.

BALEEN WHALES

ALL WHALES

ANATOMY:
THE KILLER WHALE

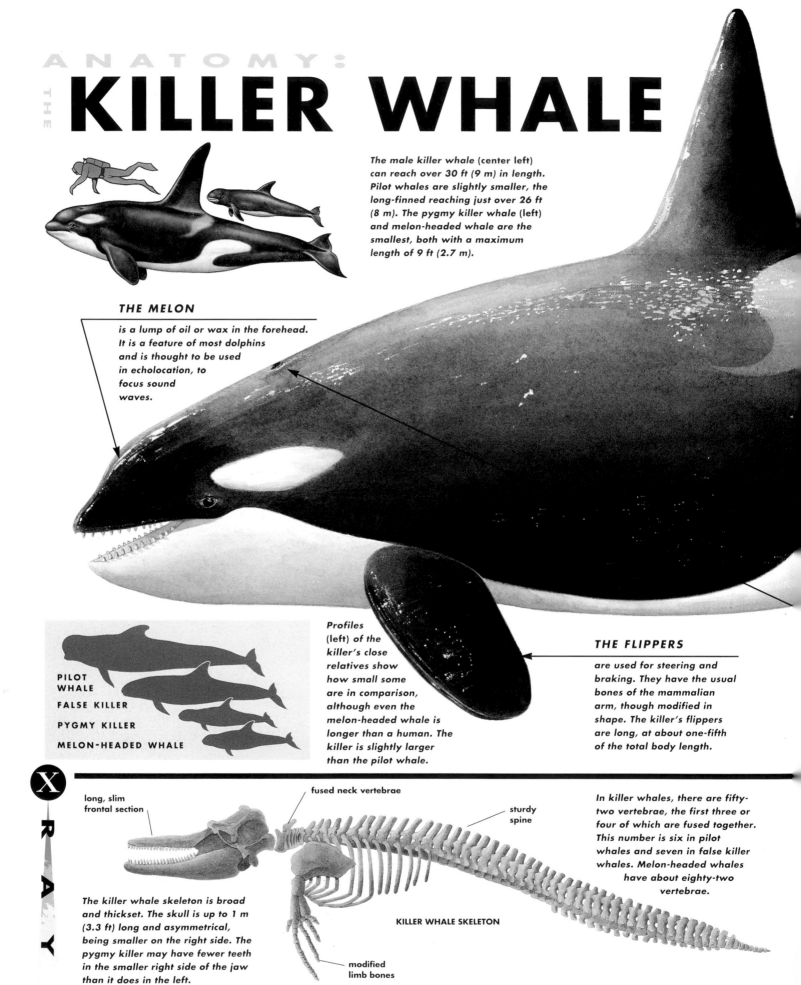

The male killer whale (center left) can reach over 30 ft (9 m) in length. Pilot whales are slightly smaller, the long-finned reaching just over 26 ft (8 m). The pygmy killer whale (left) and melon-headed whale are the smallest, both with a maximum length of 9 ft (2.7 m).

THE MELON

is a lump of oil or wax in the forehead. It is a feature of most dolphins and is thought to be used in echolocation, to focus sound waves.

PILOT WHALE
FALSE KILLER
PYGMY KILLER
MELON-HEADED WHALE

Profiles (left) of the killer's close relatives show how small some are in comparison, although even the melon-headed whale is longer than a human. The killer is slightly larger than the pilot whale.

THE FLIPPERS

are used for steering and braking. They have the usual bones of the mammalian arm, though modified in shape. The killer's flippers are long, at about one-fifth of the total body length.

X RAY

long, slim frontal section

fused neck vertebrae

sturdy spine

In killer whales, there are fifty-two vertebrae, the first three or four of which are fused together. This number is six in pilot whales and seven in false killer whales. Melon-headed whales have about eighty-two vertebrae.

KILLER WHALE SKELETON

The killer whale skeleton is broad and thickset. The skull is up to 1 m (3.3 ft) long and asymmetrical, being smaller on the right side. The pygmy killer may have fewer teeth in the smaller right side of the jaw than it does in the left.

modified limb bones

DORSAL FINS

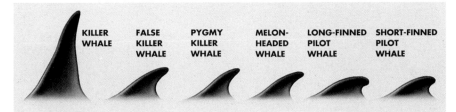

KILLER WHALE   FALSE KILLER WHALE   PYGMY KILLER WHALE   MELON-HEADED WHALE   LONG-FINNED PILOT WHALE   SHORT-FINNED PILOT WHALE

The killer's dorsal fin is the largest and most upright of any dolphin or whale, up to 6.5 ft (2 m) tall in some

mature males. This has led to common names such as épée de mer ("sword of the sea") in

French and swaardvis ("swordfish") in Dutch. The female's fin is smaller and more curved.

THE SADDLE

is a paler, grayish patch on the back just behind the dorsal fin.

THE BODY SHAPE

may not look very streamlined, but this natural torpedo is superbly designed for moving rapidly through the water.

THE BLOWHOLE

represents the nostrils, through which the whale breathes. The whale can expel stale air from its lungs and take in fresh air when almost all of its body is under water. Odontocetes have a single blowhole, while mysticetes have a double hole.

THE SKIN

is virtually hairless to improve streamlining. The insulating function of fur, to keep in body warmth, is taken over by a thick layer of fat, called blubber, underneath the skin.

THE FLUKES

are broad lobes filled with muscle and fibrous tissue. Powerful muscles pulling on the backbone swish the flukes up and down, to propel the whale. (Fishes' tails move from side to side.)

FACT FILE:
THE KILLER WHALE

CLASSIFICATION

GENUS: *ORCINUS*

SPECIES: *ORCA*

SIZE

FULL LENGTH/MALE: 21–32 FT (6.5–9.8 M)

FULL LENGTH/FEMALE: 20–26 FT (6–8 M)

WEIGHT/MALE: 4–9 TONS

WEIGHT/FEMALE: 2.5–3.5 TONS

COLORATION

BLACK BACK, SIDES, DORSAL FIN, FLIPPERS, AND UPPER FLUKES; WHITE CHIN, THROAT, BELLY, AND UNDER-FLUKES. TWO WHITE LOBES ALONG THE LOWER FLANKS BEHIND THE DORSAL FIN, TWO WHITE OVAL FLASHES BEHIND AND SLIGHTLY ABOVE THE EYES (THESE VARY IN POSITION WITH THE GEOGRAPHICAL LOCATION), AND GRAY SADDLE BEHIND DORSAL FIN. OCCASIONALLY PURE BLACK ALL OVER, OR EVEN ALBINO WHITE

FEATURES

SLEEK, MUSCULAR, THICKSET SHAPE

BLUNTISH HEAD WITH PROTRUDING FOREHEAD LUMP OR MELON

There are usually 11 teeth in each half of each jaw, though the number varies from 10 to 14. They are cone-shaped and pointed, oval in cross section, and angle back a little down the gullet. They interlock when the jaws close. The melon-headed whales have up to 100 teeth.

KILLER WHALE SKULL

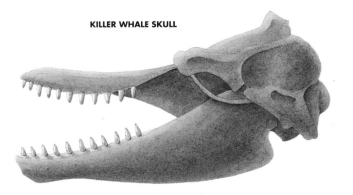

Cross section of a whale tooth. From the lines on the tooth, scientists are able to tell the age of the animal.

LORDS OF THE OCEANS

A POD OR GROUP OF KILLER WHALES SURGING THROUGH THE SEA IS AN UNFORGETTABLE SIGHT. REACHING SPEEDS OF 35 MILES (55 KILOMETERS) AN HOUR, THEY ARE AMONG THE FASTEST OF ALL CETACEANS

What does a killer whale do all day? It swims around. It rests. It leaps out of the water from time to time. It talks with its comembers in the group, or pod. In fact, we have a distorted view of the killer whale's day, because most of the time we can observe only from above water.

These whales spend much of their time actively searching for food below the surface, out of our sight. They can hunt by sound, using echolocation, so feeding goes on at night as well as by day; feeding is linked more to the tides than to light and dark. One research study estimated that killer whales spent half of their time traveling, looking for, and eating food; about 20 percent in more "playful" feeding, involving acrobatics; around 12

> DALL'S PORPOISE IS THE ONLY CETACEAN THAT CAN MATCH THE KILLER WHALE FOR SPEED

percent in rest and sleep; a similar proportion in obvious play; and a few percent in touching, sliding against, and nuzzling each other.

There is little natural danger for an adult killer whale. All members of the pod keep a lookout for trouble and warn each other of threats. Even a great white shark rarely attacks. And anyway, an adult killer whale is as large as, and can swim faster than, a great white or any other meat-eating shark. Only a few ultrastreamlined fish, such as the sailfish, swordfish, and marlin, can swim faster.

Killer whales keep an eye on above-water action by spy-hopping. They can maintain this pose for many minutes, seemingly stationary in the water as though standing on the bottom, with the waves lapping around them.

Like many other whales, killers breach—leap clear of the water and then splash back in, usually on their sides. There are several explanations for breaching. It may be a visual or sound signal to others in the pod, or to strangers from another pod. It may be to rid the skin of pests and parasites. It may be to scare and herd prey when hunting. Or it may be simply for fun.

Killer whales also porpoise—swim speedily just below the surface, leap out above the water in an almost horizontal trajectory, then dip back in, and so on. Old-time mariners, mending their sailcloth with needle and thread, used to remark that the whales looked as though they were trying to "sew sky and sea together."

Pilot whales make long feeding dives of up to ten minutes before they surface to blow (above).

A killer whale (below) *spy-hopping to see what is happening above water.*

Henry Ausloos/NHPA

A killer whale (left) *in the cold waters of Glacier Bay, Alaska. Killers live in all the world's oceans.*

Unlike many larger whales, killer whales do not make seasonal or habitual migrations. They may travel to follow food sources, which sometimes vary seasonally. The members of the pod swim abreast roughly in line, rarely spreading out for more than one-third mile. Their usual traveling speed is 6–9 mph (10–15 km/h), and they can easily cover 62 miles (100 km) in a day.

DIVING ABILITIES

When moving slowly or searching for food, the killer whale has a distinctive diving pattern. It makes a series of short dives, around four or five, each lasting up to half a minute. Between each dive the whale surfaces to blow, or breathe. The warm, moist, exhaled air rushes out like a burst of steam, mixed with an aerosol of mucus droplets from the linings of the lungs and airways.

After this series of shorter dives, the killer whale then dives for a longer period, from five to ten minutes. Most of the dives are fairly shallow. The whales have no natural need to go deeper, since their food does not. However, trained whales have dived to below 1,640 ft (500 m).

Pilot whales are also fast movers, swimming at almost 32 mph (50 km/h) when alarmed. They can dive deeply, too, reaching depths greater than 3,280 ft (1,000 m). Like killer whales, they spy-hop. If there is something of interest above the surface, the pilot whale may roll over onto its side, so that it gets a good view with one eye. ∎

HABITATS

François Gohier/Ardea

Between them, the globicephalids live in almost every part of every ocean in the world. However, this widespread global distribution shows many local variations. The great killer whale is truly cosmopolitan: It has been sighted from the Arctic to the Antarctic, in the Atlantic, Pacific, and Indian Oceans. However, it shows a preference for coastal areas and cooler, shallower waters, including bays and estuaries. Killers can even leave the saltwater of the ocean and swim through estuaries up into rivers, though they rarely range very far into freshwater.

The killers may venture among the loose ice floes of the polar waters, searching for food such as seals and even polar bears. However, the denser the ice cover becomes, the less frequent the killer whales. Since they track the edges of the ice fields,

Killer whales (above) *frequently swim just under the surface of the water, leaving only their long dorsal fins exposed from above.*

A male killer whale breaching (right). *In the final stage, the whale's body will be entirely clear of the water in a straight, horizontal line.*

Because of their similarities in coloration and shape, it is not easy to distinguish between species of pilot and killer whales (with the exception of the orca with its long dorsal fin) and some dolphins, making accurate distribution maps difficult.

Up until about thirty years ago sightings of false killers were rare, but since then scientists have learned more about the habits of all the species, enabling us to construct a more accurate picture of their whereabouts.

KEY

GREAT KILLER WHALE

SHORT-FINNED PILOT WHALE
MELON-HEADED WHALE
PYGMY KILLER WHALE
FALSE KILLER WHALE

LONG-FINNED PILOT WHALE

KEY FACTS

● **Every single species of whales and dolphins has been known to strand or beach on the shore. Out of the water, which supports and buoys up the body weight, a whale soon suffocates under the weight of its own body.**

● **False killer whales have sometimes been seen swimming with dolphins, such as gray dolphins, with which they are often confused. Long-finned pilots sometimes travel with common and bottle-nosed dolphins. Short-finned pilot whales have been seen in mixed groups with bottle-nosed or Pacific white-sided dolphins.**

● **Pilot whales strand more often, and in greater numbers, than any other cetacean. False killer whales also strand frequently, while the killer whale and pygmy killer rarely strand.**

Ken Balcons/Bruce Coleman Ltd.

DISTRIBUTION

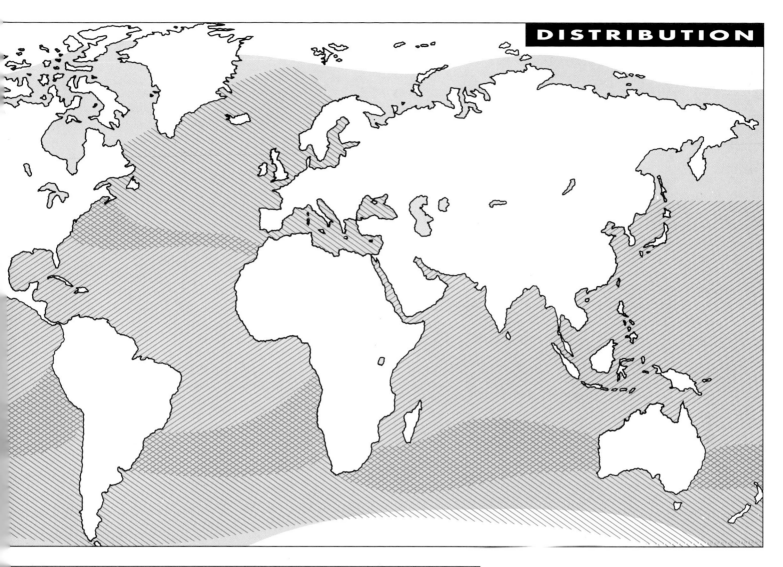

they move closer to the pole in spring and back toward temperate regions in autumn—simply following the retreat and advance of the ice. They are attracted to the polar regions because these waters are proportionally more productive in terms of life forms (cooler water contains more oxygen). The polar seas are especially rich in summer, when nutrients well up from the depths of the sea. The killer whales are at the summit of many food chains, so they are dependent on the rich web of life below them.

OTHER KILLERS

False killer whales live in all tropical, subtropical, and warm temperate waters. They tend to occur in the middle of the oceans. However, they have been seen in the Mediterranean Sea, Red Sea, and other partly enclosed seas.

False killers are fairly easy to identify by their habit of riding in the bow wave of a ship and their extraordinary porpoising abilities; it is also not difficult to locate them. They are the largest whales to enjoy bow-riding, but are also relatively slow. Any vessel going much faster than about 15 mph (25 km/h) will leave them behind—though they can still be seen playfully leaping in the waves of the ship's wake. They are very noisy, vocal whales. Their piercing whistles can be heard hundreds of yards away, even above the throb of a ship's engines.

The pygmy killer whale is even more at home far from land, in warmer, deeper seas than either of its larger relatives. It seems to occur in deeper tropical oceans all around the world. The pygmy killer's avoidance of land means that it rarely enters partly enclosed seas, although there have been some sightings in the Mediterranean.

Long-finned pilot whales like the cool, deep waters of temperate seas, whereas short-finned ones prefer tropical and subtropical regions. The northern subspecies of long-fins, *melaena*, lives in the North Atlantic. The southern subspecies, *edwardi*, inhabits the South Atlantic, South Pacific, and southern Indian Ocean. They seem to stay mainly within areas with a water temperature of 55–82°F (13–28°C).

Melon-headed whales probably live in all tropical and subtropical seas. However, less is known about this species than the others. At sea, they can be hard to distinguish from pygmy killers. At closer range, they lack the white "goatee" that the pygmy killer sports on its lower lip and chin. ■

FOCUS ON

THE BAY OF PLENTY

For many years, killer whales have been sighted and monitored around the coasts of New Zealand. There are common sightings off Milford Sound in the southwest and Kaikoura in the northeast of South Island. Killers are seen virtually all year round in the wide, sweeping Bay of Plenty on the northeastern coast of North Island. These locations have one major feature in common: a richness of sea life, especially squid and fish, encouraged by the right combinations of water currents, nutrient availability, and seabed topography.

In the summer, warm ocean currents circulating counterclockwise from the tropical Pacific to the northeast bring schools of squid, fish, and other food. In the winter, the cooler waters of the Southern Current flow around New Zealand from the west. But the Bay of Plenty is largely sheltered from its effects, so life continues to thrive. There are resident pods of killer whales here, as there are off the coasts of British Columbia in Canada. The pods congregate when their food is concentrated, such as a school of fish or squid, or they spread out to forage for more scattered prey.

OCEAN CURRENTS

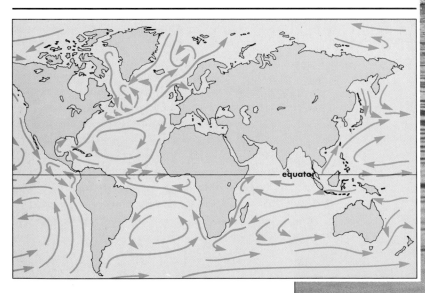

The surface ocean currents swirl clockwise in the Northern Hemisphere and counterclockwise in the Southern Hemisphere. Around New Zealand a warm current flows from the north between Australia and New Zealand and a cold current, called the West Drift, sweeps from west to east to the south of the islands. Because of the warm current, the North Island of New Zealand enjoys Mediterranean weather conditions.

NEIGHBORS

The oceans around New Zealand support a rich diversity of wildlife. In the Bay of Plenty, squid and fish abound, attracting many marine animals including dolphins and seals.

WANDERING ALBATROSS

This nomadic species has the largest wingspan of any bird. It spends most of its time at sea.

RISSO'S DOLPHIN

Living in pods of about a dozen or so, these robust mammals spend most of their time in deep waters.

NEW ZEALAND'S NORTH ISLAND

North Island covers an area of 44,297 sq miles (114,729 sq km) and is smaller than South Island. The two islands are separated by Cook Strait. The center of North Island contains New Zealand's largest lake, Lake Taupo. To its south there are geysers, volcanoes, and hot springs, which make the area very unstable.

BAY OF PLENTY

NORTH ISLAND

SPERM WHALE

The largest of the toothed whales, sperm whales are found in all the world's oceans.

MARLIN

A powerful and graceful swimmer, the marlin has a reputation for being the fastest of all fish.

OCEAN SUNFISH

This fish spends most of its time eating and breeding and is probably the most fertile of all fish.

MANTA RAY

This gigantic fish feeds on the smallest of ocean life. Because it lacks teeth, its mouth acts like a sieve.

GREEN TURTLE

One of the largest turtles, this reptile's head is so big that it cannot withdraw into its shell.

Illustrations Dale Evans/Wildlife Art Agency

SOCIAL STRUCTURE

Killer whales have one of the most remarkable, cohesive, and stable social structures of any mammal. They live in extended family groups called pods. These stay together virtually for life—unlike the vast majority of other social mammals, where the young males leave and try to join other groups as they reach sexual maturity.

A pod usually consists of between five and twenty-five individuals, of three or four generations. There is usually an older female, the grandmother, who may be over fifty years old. She is accompanied by her sons and daughters, who might be in their twenties. These daughters are also accompanied by their offspring, the grandchildren. So the pod may have three or four adult males, ten to fifteen adult females, and their offspring.

Killer whale pods tend to split up when they get too large, and this seems to happen without aggression. There appears to be an optimum pod size depending on the local conditions and food availability. Pods of fewer than six animals do not usually last for long, since larger pods tend to muscle in on the best feeding sites and prey.

A pod that frequents coastal waters may roam over a basic home range of 310 miles (500 kilometers). However, some pods are probably more oceanic, with no true home base.

UNDERWATER CONVERSATION
Using water microphones called hydrophones, scientists have studied the sounds of killer whales in great detail. The sounds and calls are partly for the sonar process called echolocation. The whale beams out the sound and then listens for

David Fleetham/Oxford Scientific Films

the pattern of returning echoes, which is analyzed in the brain to give information about objects around it. The calls are for communication, too.

It is now known that each pod has its own individual accent, or dialect, of calls and songs. Human experts can learn to distinguish these, so the whales most certainly can. Neighboring pods may have some calls or call imitations in common, especially

KILLER WHALES

live in strong family groups of several generations. Although they have an awesome reputation as hunters, their protective instincts toward one another are rare among mammals.

Melon-headed whales live in groups of 20–30, but sometimes as many as 500 may be seen together in large herds.

KILLER TALK

Killer whales have a language of their own. One type of sound is the click or tick. It usually occurs as a series of short pulses, each lasting around a fraction of a second and with a wide frequency range. This is often used for echolocation, for navigation and catching prey. Another type is the tonal whistle, which can last for more than ten seconds. These sounds appear very high-pitched to our ears. A third type is screamlike of even higher frequencies, which are too high for human hearing. This sound lasts for about a second.

where their ranges overlap. But every pod retains its own distinct dialect. When a calf is born into a pod, it hears calls in this dialect all around. The details of the calls become fixed into the baby's memory, and they are retained for life. Gradually, over generations, the dialect may change and evolve as new nuances and calls are incorporated. It also seems that it is not the basic structure of the sound or call itself, but how it is made and the emphasis given, that conveys some of the information.

SKILLS AND TRADITIONS

Each pod also has its own favorite prey animals and favorite places and methods of hunting them. It also has traditional resting sites and play places, where pod members rub and massage their bodies on the pebbly bed or among the fronds of kelp. These skills, techniques, and sites are passed by the collective memory through the generations.

Far less is known about the other two species of killer whales. False killers travel in small groups, which are part of a larger herd. The groups are mixed in terms of age and sex, and they use many and varied high-pitched vocalizations. The shy pygmy killers laze around in small groups of ten to fifty by day, spy-hopping and resting. ■

PILOT PODS

Doug Perrine/Planet Earth Pictures

Long-finned pilot whales live as close-knit groups of six or more, with an internal hierarchy of seniority. Young males bear the scars of aggression when they are forced by others to leave the group, with jaw-clapping as a threat display. The members of the group sometimes float haphazardly at the surface, with flippers and fins showing and touching one another—apparently asleep. Many groups may join to form much larger herds of hundreds usually for traveling, with the large males in the lead.

Short-finned pilots live in strongly bonded groups of ten or more. These may swim as part of a larger herd, hundreds strong. They often help their injured or exhausted colleagues by supporting them at the surface so that they can breathe.

Illustration Steve Roberts/Wildlife Art Agency

HUNTING

If you want to know what a killer whale eats, the short answer is almost everything that the oceans have to offer. Killer whales have been studied at several sites around the world. Each study reveals different preferred prey and hunting methods, depending on the season and the availability of food. In some cases, the whales hunt individually. In others, the members of a pod cooperate as a team. In others, several pods come together and feed communally with little aggression.

One important point is that the whales must remember the times and locations of good feeding sites as part of the pod's collected body of knowledge. A second point is that the killer whale is the only cetacean that habitually takes warm-blooded prey—that is, birds and mammals.

WHALES AROUND THE WORLD

A brief trip around the world shows how killer whales hunt certain kinds of prey. But these are well-documented study cases, within relatively easy reach of land and, therefore, scientists and equipment. Wandering pods of killers in the middle of the ocean may have very different habits.

Off the coasts of Washington State and British Columbia fairly resident pods of killer whales have been monitored for thirty years. Whales and fishermen gather for the annual run of salmon making their way along the shore and up into the rivers to spawn. About sixteen pods come to

BEACH SNATCH

Killers have learned how to beach themselves to grab a sea lion pup on the waterline. In the process the whale may be left high and dry, but the feast is worth the risks involved.

Jeff Foott Productions/Survival Anglia

A large male killer whale in cold water can eat up to 220 lb (100 kg) a day, the equivalent of three or four seal pups or 400 herring.

Illustrations Robin Boutell

SALMON RUN

When cooperating to catch salmon (above), the killers' first tactic is to swim after the fish in a line. When the salmon are where they want them, the killers arc around the school and pick the fish off one by one as they try to escape.

in SIGHT

THE KILLER'S MENU

Killer whales eat almost anything that swims in the sea. However, the pods in each area have their own traditional types of prey and hunting methods, so no single killer whale is likely to sample the entire menu.

   These are some of the more documented delicacies:

- Bony fish, such as salmon, herring, tuna, cod, and many others
- Cartilaginous fish, such as skates, rays, and sharks
- Squid and cuttlefish
- Seals and sea lions, including gray, common, and elephant seals and California and Steller's sea lions
- Walruses
- Manatees and dugongs
- Penguins, such as the jackass and king
- Other seabirds, such as gulls, frigate birds, and boobies
- Dolphins, such as the spinner
- Porpoises, such as the common and Dall's
- Medium-sized whales, such as beluga and narwhal
- Large whales, such as the blue, humpback, gray, and many others, including their calves
- Sea turtles, especially the leatherback
- The occasional polar bear

one salmon channel. The water is murky, so eyesight is not very useful for long-distance location of the salmon. The killer whales use their echolocating sonar, sending out streams of clicks with a relatively low frequency, unlike the high ultrasonic echolocation pulses of dolphins.

The killers listen to the returning echoes, waiting for the characteristic sonar signature produced by sound rebounding from a salmon school. The killers also listen to the sounds and echoes produced by other pod members and by nearby pods.

INDIVIDUAL AND TEAM PURSUIT

One hunting strategy is for each killer whale to select and chase its own prey fish individually. Salmon are a considerable size, and this makes the individual pursuit a worthwhile tactic. Once a killer gets close to some fish, it turns off its sonar and uses vision to make the final lunge and catch. The fish is swallowed in one gulp, as the killer's mouth is not designed for chewing.

There are also other variations for the salmon hunt. They may hunt as a group (see artwork caption, page 2281). When each pod member has caught a fish, they all dive and resurface at a different point to continue the hunt.

WHALE KILLER

Kenneth W. Fink/Arcea

The killer whale's name probably arose from its predatory behavior and its reputation as a whale- and seal-killer. It risks its life to take sea lions from the shore (*above*), and working cooperatively will attack the much larger baleen whales, such as the humpback, fin, and even blue whale.

HERRING SCOOP

To catch fish smaller than salmon, the pod works as a team to save energy. The fish school, widely spaced at first, is circled like a caribou is surrounded by wolves, until the fish, panicked by the flashing white patches of the whales, close ranks near the surface (below). *Some whales swim into the middle of the bunch and flick their tails* (right), *producing pressure waves like gunshots in the water that stun the fish. The whales quietly move in to pick off the dazed, drifting fish.*

| BLUEFIN TUNA | COMMON SEAL | SQUID | JACKASS PENGUIN | FRIGATE BIRD |

Illustrations Ruth Grewcock

Illustrations Lee Gibbon/Wildlife Art Agency

LEATHERBACK

In Norway, millions of herring come into the fjords to shelter for the winter. Large pods of up to fifty killer whales gather for the rich pickings.

SEAL AND PENGUIN PATROL

Some groups of killer whales have become famous for their spectacular hunts of warm-blooded prey, chiefly seals and penguins. The Crozet Islands in the southern Indian Ocean, far to the southeast of Africa's southern tip, are rocky, remote, and gale-lashed. But in spring, about fifteen to twenty pods of killer whales arrive for their traditional feast. The islands' more sheltered beaches are crowded with breeding penguins, such as the king penguin, and breeding seals, such as the elephant seal.

As the seal pups and penguin chicks grow up, their parents leave. Most of the parents are experienced enough to note the tall triangular fins of the killer whales patrolling just offshore. But the youngsters are less lucky. As they leave the nursery beaches and take to the sea, the killers snap them up. Even on land, the seals are not safe. But beach-snatching is a risky method, as there is always a chance that the whale will be truly stranded.

Killers teach their youngsters the technique of beaching, pushing them into the shallows. When a whale has caught a seal, it may play with its injured victim. It tosses the pup into the air by its mouth or tail, or clouts and bats it with flippers or flukes, like a cat playing with a crippled mouse.

SLIPPERY SLIDE TO DEATH

Among the ice floes of polar regions, killer whales swim under the floes or lean on them to make them tilt and tip. Seals resting on the floe slide straight into the mouths of waiting pod members.

False killer whales feed on squid and large fish, such as tuna and bonito. They shake the fish to remove head and skin before swallowing. They also hold fish for their young to nibble, and they are infamous for stealing fish from fishing lines.

Pygmy killer whales feed mostly at night, presumably on fish and perhaps squid. Melon-headed whales also probably have fish as their main food item. The pilot whales use echolocation when feeding; they take a lot of squid. The short-finned pilot hunts by night. The long-finned pilot also eats fish, such as cod, horse mackerel, and turbot. ■

WHALE KILLERS

ALTHOUGH KILLINGS CONTINUE, PUBLIC OPINION IS NOW FIRMLY IN FAVOR OF PROTECTING WHALES—BUT ARE WE ABUSING OUR NEWFOUND FRIENDSHIP WITH THESE INTELLIGENT GIANTS?

N one of the six whale species covered in this issue is in imminent danger. Most are oceanic, so they rarely come into contact with people. They are at some risk from pollution, since these whales are at the top of the food chain. Any pollutants tend to get more and more concentrated as they get farther up the food chains. This problem, not unique to killer whales, faces many large oceanic predators.

The great problem for whale conservationists is that whales and dolphins are difficult to count. They roam over large areas and stay submerged for long periods. As a result, estimates of population sizes vary enormously, even when carried out by reputable scientific surveys. There are hardly any global population estimates for the species; the largest numbers of killer whales are thought to be in the southern waters around the Antarctic, with rough estimates of 100,000–200,000 individuals.

KILLER WHALES HAVE LONG BEEN SEEN AS A THREAT TO HUMANS, BUT THEY ARE INFINITELY LESS DEADLY THAN SHARKS

LOVE AND HATE

People have had a love-hate relationship with killer whales for many years. Thousands want to see them performing in captivity; thousands of others do not—they want the whales set free. Others, however, would rather see them dead.

Some whalers found killer whales a nuisance because they tore up the carcasses of giant whales waiting to be hauled into the factory ships or shore stations. Others looked upon them as allies in the hunt for great whales and even shared the catch with them. Killers themselves have been taken by whalers in Greenland, Norway, and Japan for their flesh and blubber and oil, but usually as a secondary

target if little else is available. In some areas, killer whales are killed by fishermen, who claim that the whales take the herring, salmon, and other fish stocks. In the 1950s the United States forces apparently shot hundreds of killer whales at the request of the Icelandic government to protect fish stocks.

The numbers of killer whales taken live, for captivity, are probably approaching a mere 200. They receive much publicity, but this is not a threat to the overall populations. It remains true that there are hardly any reported attacks by killer whales on humans. Those that do happen are usually the result of extreme provocation or mistaken identity. One expert remarked, "My orcas are far safer than my pet dogs."

False killer whales are also thought to be fairly common in some areas. They have been killed in Japan by being driven ashore. At one time they

Mysteriously beached, pilot whales throng on Tasmania, off mainland Australia (above).

Henry Ausloos/NHPA

Anthony Joyce/Planet Earth Pictures

THEN & NOW

This map shows the location of oil slicks visible from space in the late 1980s.

More than 3.3 million tons of oil contaminate the world's oceans each year. Much of it is deliberately dumped—both from the shore and from tankers flushing out their holds. The *Exxon Valdez* incident in 1989 affected nearly 500 miles (800 km) of Alaskan coastline and caused the deaths of many otters, seabirds, and killer whales. But the smaller spills, too, can cause huge environmental damage. Heavy metals, such as mercury and cadmium, and chemicals such as pesticides, are also proving lethal to oceanic wildlife.

were captured by Arab nations, who traded their teeth with the North American Indians. They are notorious for stealing fish from lines and are sometimes shot or speared for this crime. False killer whales occasionally become ensnared in tuna nets, especially in the tropical eastern Pacific, and die by drowning. And they are also lured by the dolphins and porpoises entangled in these nets, apparently having a liking for warm-blooded prey like their larger relative. However, in the artificial and frantic conditions of the tuna nets, it is difficult to see who is attacking whom.

NAVY WHALES

Pygmy killer whales have been taken into captivity but show marked aggression, both to people and other animals in their tanks. This is most unusual among the whale and dolphin group. Pilot whales

Sunlight dapples the back of a short-finned pilot whale off the Canary island of Tenerife.

ALONGSIDE MAN

STAR PERFORMERS

Captive killer whales have thrilled crowds since the first oceanarium opened in Florida in 1938. People were amazed to see how docile and friendly the killer was, and thrilled at its tricks.

But such enterprises draw criticism. Killers rarely breed successfully in captivity; they also do not live long. The tall dorsal fin flops down toward the body. Also the killers are often trained to live alongside dolphins, which they normally include among their prey. The stresses of a captive lifestyle and abnormal relationships lead to gastric ulcers.

British Film Institute/Warner Bros. Ltd.

and other tank-mates show fright reactions to the pygmy killers and have been attacked and killed.

The intelligence and docility of killer and pilot whales have led to their appearance in captivity and also to their use by various navies. The whales learn to attach mines to enemy vessels and to pick up lost devices, such as torpedoes, from the seabed, using a special harness with a grabber attached.

MYSTERIOUS MASS DEATHS

More pilot whales are found stranded than any other whale. Most are whole herds of apparently healthy animals; occasionally a sick animal drifts in alone. It is still not clear why this happens. If the living animals are pushed or towed or herded back out to sea, they often come straight back in again. In Newfoundland, the whales may follow migrating young squid inshore and strand in this way.

The film Free Willy *(above) told the story of a captive killer whale—its poor living conditions, its bond with a boy, and the promise of release.*

After rescuing a beached short-finned whale, volunteer biologists in Florida draw a blood sample from its fin (below).

Doug Perrine/Planet Earth Pictures

Pilot whales were killed in large numbers during the heyday of whaling. The main products were meat for people and their domestic animals and oil from the blubber and bulbous head. About 40,000 pilots were taken from the west Atlantic in the 1950s, following the establishment of a whaling base in Newfoundland. The population in the North Atlantic collapsed. Between 1962 and 1973, the number fell to less than 7,000. Hopefully, with the cessation of commercial whaling in the 1980s, it will recover. In world terms, however, both species of pilot whales are certainly not rare.

THE FAEROES WHALE KILL

Long-finned pilot whales have been caught by Faeroe Islanders every year for about four centuries in a traditional festival. The meat and blubber helped the islanders survive. Boats drive the whales to the shore, where they are hacked to death in the shallows by waiting islanders. Whole families, including children, take part in the killing.

Today the islands are in little need of the whale products, since they have income from fishing. Furthermore, some of the whale offal is contaminated with the heavy-metal pollutant mercury and so cannot be eaten; it is simply dumped in the sea. But the Faeroes still see the deaths of 2,500 whales every year, which is now the largest whale kill in the Northern Hemisphere. The kill is still deemed traditional and therefore outside the international whaling restrictions (see Into the Future, page 2289).

In Japan and the Antilles, short-finned pilot whales are sometimes taken by driving them onshore. However, like the long-finned pilot whale kills, this poses more a question for personal taste and morality than for the survival of the whales. It presents no great threat to their overall populations. ∎

INTO THE FUTURE

The International Whaling Commission (IWC) was set up in 1946 to monitor and regulate whaling—chiefly of the large baleen whales—on a global basis. By the early 1980s, public opinion was turning against whaling. In 1982, the member nations of the IWC voted to ban all commercial whaling after 1985. It was billed as a moratorium, a pause to see what would happen. Norway and Japan, as major whaling countries, objected.

The IWC regularly reviews its ban, with much heated debate. Some nations want to resume controlled hunting of some species. Other nations wish to keep the ban and extend it to smaller whales, such as the killer whales, dolphins, and porpoises. The IWC Scientific Committee compiles reports on whales and their populations, and both pro- and anti-whalers produce other scientific evidence to support their cases.

PREDICTION

STATUS UNKNOWN

The killer and pilot whales are not substantially threatened, but their habitats continue to be polluted and many animals are still killed—either deliberately or accidentally in fishnets. Further monitoring is needed to assess their status.

There are also many smaller, nongovernmental organizations that act on behalf of cetaceans. The International Dolphin Watch (IDW) links people with an interest in dolphins, orcas, and related species. The Whale and Dolphin Conservation Society fights for the protection of whales and dolphins around the world. It aims to change both public opinion and government policies in order to bring an end to whaling. ∎

ADOPT A WHALE

The Whale and Dolphin Conservation Society is especially active in monitoring the welfare of captive cetaceans, including killer whales, and also in raising public awareness of their plight. The funds they raise are put toward whale research.

To this end, the society organizes a project to adopt cetaceans, specifically killer whales, off British Columbia, Canada. Subscribers are called adoptive parents and become Friends of the Orcas. They receive a certificate and photograph of their whale and a letter about its recent activities. The prospective candidates for adoption are described in this manner: "A25 Sharky, adult female, born 1971. Named after the distinctive shape of her dorsal fin. She has a calf, Spike, born in 1986."

THREATENED SPECIES

CITES is the Convention on International Trade in Endangered Species, opened in 1974 for signing by nations throughout the world. It is an official body for global legislation concerning wildlife protection. All cetaceans—whales, dolphins, and porpoises—are listed in the CITES Appendices (lists). International trade in these species or their products is legal only with special licenses and permission.

The International Union for the Conservation of Nature (IUCN), or the World Conservation Union, produces official lists of threatened animals in their Red Data Book. The whales in this issue, including the three species of killer whales, two species of pilot whales, and the melon-headed whale, are all listed in Category K: "Insufficiently known." This means that they are suspected to be in one of the threatened categories—rare, vulnerable, or endangered—but there is not enough information for a more precise rating.

Illustration Steve Kingston

RIGHT WHALES

Right whales are members of the baleen whales suborder Mysticeti. Other baleen whales include:

BLUE WHALE

HUMPBACK WHALE

GRAY WHALE

FIN WHALE

SEI WHALE

BRYDE'S WHALE

François Gohier/Ardea

MARINE MAMMOTHS

BEFORE HUMAN DOMINATION OF THE SEAS, RIGHT WHALES WERE ANALOGOUS TO THE WOOLLY MAMMOTHS OF THE CONTINENTS. OVER THE CENTURIES THEY WERE HUNTED VIRTUALLY TO EXTINCTION FOR HUMAN NEED—AND HUMAN GREED

S ome creatures have the bad luck to be in the wrong place at the wrong time. In one case, these two wrongs made a right—the right whales, so named because they were once the "right" whales to catch. Cruising slowly in the surface waters of the Atlantic Ocean, these huge beasts were easy and profitable targets for the first whaling fleets of sailing ships, from as early as the 12th century. Right whales were the first large seagoing victims of human killing technology, echoing the demise of woolly mammoths and other huge land herbivores 10,000 years ago.

By the late 19th century, when whalers were using explosive harpoons and fast catcher ships, the right whales had already been hunted to oblivion in most areas. The hunters' sights turned on other species: humpbacks, sperm whales, blues, and fins. It is hoped that the moratorium on commercial whaling, and the setting aside of ocean areas as màrine sanctuaries, will help their numbers recover at last.

CLASSIFICATION

Right whales belong to the cetacean order, which includes all whales, dolphins, and porpoises. There are two suborders of cetaceans: toothed whales, including the porpoises, dolphins, killer whales, sperm whales, and beaked whales; and the whalebone or baleen whales, which include the six species of rorquals, the gray whale, and the right whales.

ORDER

Cetacea
(whales and dolphins)

SUBORDER

Mysticeti
(baleen whales)

FAMILY

Balaenidae
(right and bowhead whales)

GENUS

Balaena

SPECIES

glacialis
(right whale)

mysticetus
(bowhead)

GENUS AND SPECIES

Caperea marginata
(pygmy right whale)

2291

There are three main kinds of right whales. These are the right whale itself, also called the great or common right whale or the black whale; the bowhead or Greenland right whale; and the pygmy right whale. They belong to the baleen group of whales, named after the fringes inside their mouths that are used for filtering small items of food from seawater. Other baleen whales include the slimmer, speedy rorquals—the blue, fin, sei, Bryde's, minke, and humpback—and the gray whale.

The scarcity of right whales means that we know little about their lifestyle. Even the classification of right whales invites argument. Those zoologists who opt for as few groups as possible place the three species in one family, Balaenidae. Other zoologists limit the family Balaenidae to the bowhead and a single species of right whale, with the northern and southern right whales as subspecies. The pygmy right whale is given its own family, Neobalaenidae. Still other experts prefer to describe four species in two families, as shown in the family tree (see page 2294).

THE RIGHT NAME?

Pliny the Elder (A.D. 23–79) first described the right whales in his immense multivolume encyclopedia of the ancient world, *Historia Naturalis*. In the mid-18th century, Swedish taxonomist Carl Linnaeus named the bowhead *Balaena mysticetus*, and eighteen years later, the German naturalist Fritz Müller proposed that the blackcap or ice-whale was

François Gohier/Ardea

Right whales seem to delight in lob-tailing— smacking their tail flukes on the water (above).

François Gohier/Ardea

(in)SIGHT

HOW MANY SPECIES?

There are two populations of the right whale in the world's seas, one in each hemisphere. Are these populations separate subspecies, or even separate species? Zoologists have long debated this question.

In 1822, French physiologist Antoine Desmoulins was sent a skeleton of the southern right whale from near South Africa. Not having another right whale skeleton handy for comparison, he named it *Balaena australis*; *auster* is Latin for "south." But subsequent studies failed to find significant differences between this and the northern species, *Balaena glacialis*. Indeed, there seem to be no important anatomical differences between the two.

So some modern experts say that all right whales, northern and southern, belong to a single species; there are no subspecies. Others give the northern and southern populations subspecies distinction because of the minor differences arising from some geographical isolation; they call the northern right whale *Balaena glacialis* and the southern *B. glacialis australis*.

another separate species, which he christened *Balaena glacialis*. In 1864, the British Museum decided that the right whale was different enough from its relatives to have its own genus, *Eubalaena* (*Eu* is a Greek word meaning "right").

With increasing knowledge, it was realized that the bowhead was similar enough to the right whale to belong in the same genus, which was called either *Eubalaena* or *Balaena*. One modern naming scheme now reseparates the bowhead and the two species of right whale—if they exist—into two genera, as described on the next two pages.

BIG MOUTHS

Whatever the classification, right whales are baleen whales. They eat plankton by skimming open-mouthed through the water, rather than gulping like their rorqual cousins. The narrow upper jaw or rostrum is arched upward and carries the very long baleen plates, while the lower lips extend upward to cover the baleen, giving the whale a somewhat oddlooking grin. The mouth is huge, and the head is perhaps one-third of the body length.

Breaching (lunging from the water) enables a whale to see what's happening up on the surface.

(in)SIGHT

NEW CLASSIFICATION

The classification of the right whales is somewhat confusing and remains a subject of controversy to this day. This is one of the modern alternative classification schemes as used by the World Conservation Union and the International Whaling Commission (IWC):

➤ **Family Balaenidae**
Bowhead, *Balaena mysticetus*
Northern right whale, *Eubalaena glacialis*
Southern right whale, *Eubalaena glacialis australis*
➤ **Family Neobalaenidae**
Pygmy right whale, *Caperea marginata*

The right whale has growths called callosities on the front of the head. These become infested with colonies of barnacles and other crustaceans, parasitic worms, and whale lice. The callosities and the slow surface swimming allow observers to recognize right whales relatively easily. Also, the bowhead and right whales have no dorsal fins or throat grooves, unlike their rorqual relatives.

SIZE AND SHAPE

The bowhead is the largest of the right whales; up to 65 ft (20 m) long and weighing 110 tons, it has the largest head of any animal. It lives in the high Arctic Ocean, following the edge of the ice as it spreads south in winter and shrinks north in summer. It never ventures into warm water.

The right whale grows up to 55 ft (17 m) long and weighs over 55 tons. The population of each hemisphere migrates to higher latitudes to feed during its respective summer months, then travels back to warmer waters to breed during the winter.

The pygmy right whale reaches only 16 to 20 ft (5 or 6 m) in length. Unusually, it has a dorsal fin and two throat grooves. It is probably a distant relative, and is included in the right whale group for convenience. It is rarely seen and has never been a viable target for whalers. Until recently it was known only from about fifty strandings in Australia, New Zealand, and South Africa. ■

B/W illustrations Ruth Grewcock

THE RIGHT WHALES' FAMILY TREE

The family Balaenidae is one of the three families in the suborder Mysticeti, the baleen whales. The other mysticetes are the rorquals, family Balaenopteridae, and the gray whale, family Eschrichtiidae. The mysticetes belong to the order Cetacea, which encompasses all whales and dolphins.

PYGMY RIGHT WHALE
Caperea marginata
(Ca-PEH-ree-ah mar-gin-AH-tah)

The odd man out among this group, the pygmy right whale is distinctive in having a dorsal fin and two throat grooves. It is also much smaller, and its mouth is less upwardly bowed than those of the other two right whales. Its scientific name marginata refers to the dark borders on the baleen plates.

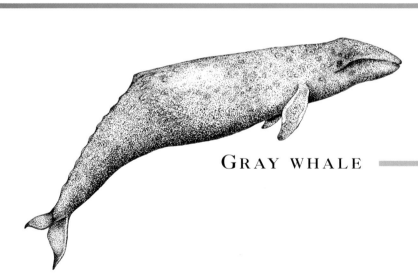

GRAY WHALE

RORQUALS
(BLUE WHALE)

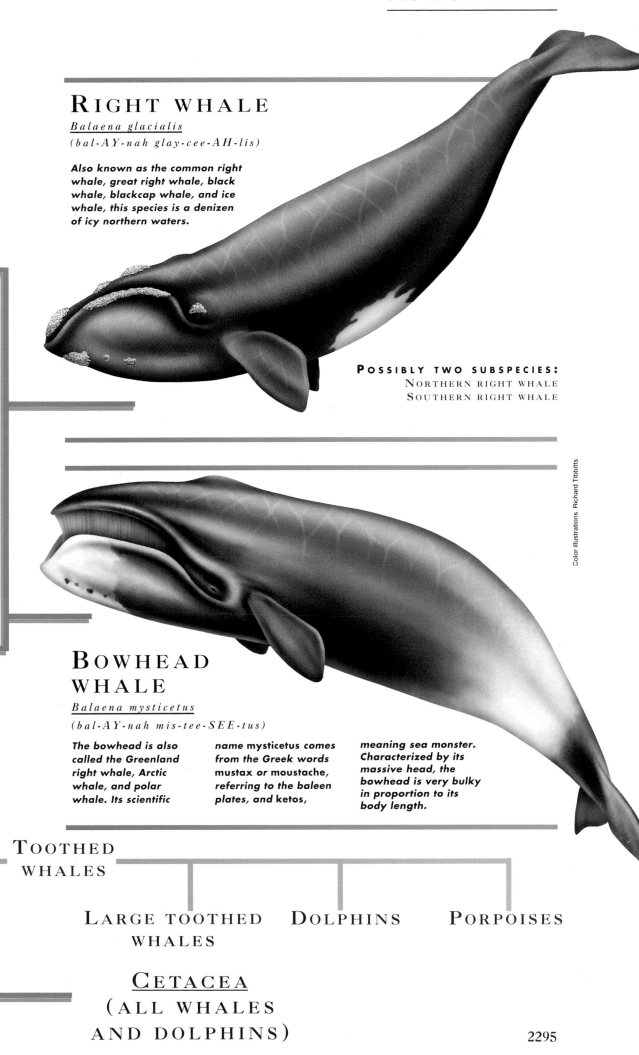

RIGHT WHALE
Balaena glacialis
(bal-AY-nah glay-cee-AH-lis)

Also known as the common right whale, great right whale, black whale, blackcap whale, and ice whale, this species is a denizen of icy northern waters.

POSSIBLY TWO SUBSPECIES:
NORTHERN RIGHT WHALE
SOUTHERN RIGHT WHALE

Color illustrations Richard Tibbitts

BOWHEAD WHALE
Balaena mysticetus
(bal-AY-nah mis-tee-SEE-tus)

The bowhead is also called the Greenland right whale, Arctic whale, and polar whale. Its scientific name mysticetus comes from the Greek words mustax or moustache, referring to the baleen plates, and ketos, meaning sea monster. Characterized by its massive head, the bowhead is very bulky in proportion to its body length.

RIGHT WHALES

BALEEN WHALES

TOOTHED WHALES

LARGE TOOTHED WHALES   DOLPHINS   PORPOISES

<u>CETACEA</u>
(ALL WHALES AND DOLPHINS)

2295

ANATOMY: THE RIGHT WHALE

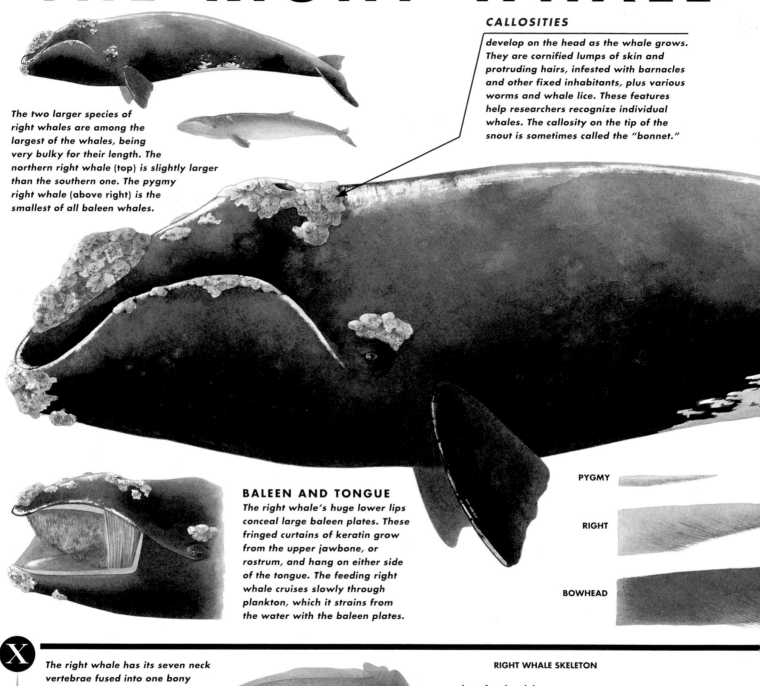

The two larger species of right whales are among the largest of the whales, being very bulky for their length. The northern right whale (top) is slightly larger than the southern one. The pygmy right whale (above right) is the smallest of all baleen whales.

CALLOSITIES

develop on the head as the whale grows. They are cornified lumps of skin and protruding hairs, infested with barnacles and other fixed inhabitants, plus various worms and whale lice. These features help researchers recognize individual whales. The callosity on the tip of the snout is sometimes called the "bonnet."

PYGMY

RIGHT

BOWHEAD

BALEEN AND TONGUE

The right whale's huge lower lips conceal large baleen plates. These fringed curtains of keratin grow from the upper jawbone, or rostrum, and hang on either side of the tongue. The feeding right whale cruises slowly through plankton, which it strains from the water with the baleen plates.

X-RAY

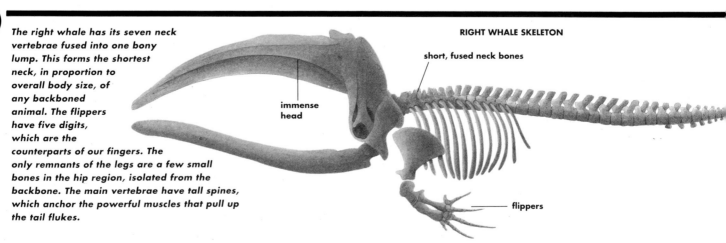

The right whale has its seven neck vertebrae fused into one bony lump. This forms the shortest neck, in proportion to overall body size, of any backboned animal. The flippers have five digits, which are the counterparts of our fingers. The only remnants of the legs are a few small bones in the hip region, isolated from the backbone. The main vertebrae have tall spines, which anchor the powerful muscles that pull up the tail flukes.

RIGHT WHALE SKELETON

short, fused neck bones

immense head

flippers

X-ray illustrations Elisabeth Smith

RIGHT WHALE **BOWHEAD WHALE** **PYGMY RIGHT WHALE**

A look at the heads of these three whales helps us tell them apart instantly. The right whale's head is encrusted with callosities. The bowhead is smooth with a white chin. The pygmy right whale has a more streamlined head with a less acute arch to the mouth.

THE BACK

lacks a dorsal fin or ridge, unlike the rorquals. The body is deep and wide, making this whale look bulky and tubby when compared to its faster rorqual relatives.

THE SKIN

is smooth and hairless and covers a thick layer of fatty blubber. It is black overall, but there may be paler patches and scars where the whale has been attacked or has fought with rivals.

THE FLUKES

push the whale through the water as they thrash up and down. They are not modified rear limbs, since they have no bones in them; they are skin-covered muscle and connective tissue. The legs have disappeared and only tiny bone remnants remain, hidden in the flesh of the body.

THE BALEEN

or whalebone (left) is not bone but the horny substance keratin, from which our fingernails are formed. It grows in plates, like long, narrow pages from a book. The inner edges fray into bristlelike fibers that filter food from the seawater.

CLASSIFICATION

GENUS: *BALAENA* (OR *EUBALAENA*)
SPECIES: *GLACIALIS*

SIZE

LENGTH/MALE: 46–60 FT (14–18 M)
LENGTH/FEMALE: 50–65 FT (15–20 M)
WEIGHT/MALE: 55–77 TONS
WEIGHT/FEMALE: 66–99 TONS
FLIPPER LENGTH: UP TO 7 FT (2.2 M)
TAIL WIDTH: UP TO 13 FT (4 M) TIP TO TIP
LENGTH AT BIRTH: 16 FT (5 M)

COLORATION

BLACK ALL OVER, WITH MOTTLED BROWNS AND A FEW PALE AREAS OR SCARS; HEAD CALLOSITIES OF VARIOUS COLORS SUCH AS CHALKY GRAY; BARNACLES; AND PALER OR WHITE PATCHES ON THE CHIN AND BELLY WHERE THE SKIN SLOUGHS

FEATURES

A BULKY, ALMOST TUBBY WHALE WITH HUGE, FLAPLIKE LOWER LIPS, EYES LOW ON THE HEAD AT THE CORNERS OF THE MOUTH, TRIANGULAR PECTORAL FINS, NARROW TAIL STOCK AND POINTED FLUKES, NO DORSAL FIN

The right whale's narrow, arched rostrum (upper jawbone) accommodates extra-long baleen plates. The lower jawbones are widely spaced; they are connected at the front by ligaments, which help pull the jaw shut.

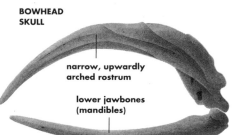

BOWHEAD SKULL

narrow, upwardly arched rostrum

lower jawbones (mandibles)

PYGMY RIGHT WHALE SKULL

The rostrum links to the skull by loose, slightly flexible joints, stabilized by huge muscles. This allows the mouth and head to absorb shocks and water pressure when skim-feeding. As in all great whales, the skull's braincase is relatively tiny.

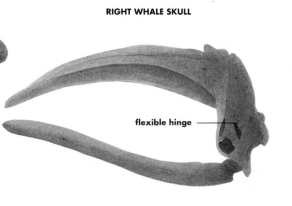

RIGHT WHALE SKULL

flexible hinge

HUGE AND UNHURRIED

OBSERVERS OF THE RIGHT WHALE HAVE DUBBED IT "THE COW OF THE SEAS," REFERRING TO THE WAY THIS BULKY AND SEEMINGLY UNINTELLIGENT BEAST REMAINS UNFLAPPABLE IN THE FACE OF HUMAN INTRUDERS

Most of the right whale's day is spent feeding, but this docile giant still finds time for rest and even play, especially when young. As whales go, it is relatively easy to approach by vessel; this was a major reason for its downfall in the heyday of whaling. For the same reason, today's right whales are popular with whale-watchers.

BASKING, ROLLING, AND DIVING

The right whale generally lives in shallow coastal waters. When the sun shines, it basks contentedly in the comparatively warm surface waters. It often half-rolls and rests belly-up, or completes several rolls in succession. Then, if not feeding, it may cruise at or just under the surface, driven by slow undulations of the tail flukes. The cruising speed is only 6 mph (10 km/h) or so, and after about ten minutes the whale takes another rest or dives. The right whale dives for ten to twenty minutes, though it can stay under for up to one hour. It has often been seen lying motionless on the seabed during these dives; what exactly it is doing is not clear.

Right whales communicate by singing, slapping the surface of the water with their fins or flukes, or breaching. This involves shooting up to the surface and bursting out of the water, then crashing back onto the surface with a 66-ton splash. Sometimes a right whale exposes its flukes to the wind, or rolls on to its side and lifts a flipper, to be blown along by the breeze, like a huge sailboard.

THE DOUBLE BLOW

While cruising along, the right whale breathes or "blows" every minute or so, rising and then diving smoothly again. The two blowholes (nostrils) are separate, and their two sprays rise in characteristic V formation up to 16 ft (5 m) into the air. The spray consists of warm air, condensing water vapor, and oily secretions from the linings of the whale's airways and lungs. The blow of this species is often highly visible since it lives in cold oceans, where the exhalation condenses thickly. Whalers used to complain that a wounded right whale, blowing heavily as it was secured for tow or hauled on board, would drench the vessel with a mist of slimy droplets.

THE BOWHEAD'S DAY

The bowhead whale lives only in the far northern oceans, which are cold all year-round. In many respects, it resembles the right whale in its daily routine. Bowheads tend to swim slowly and breathe in more rapid bursts than right whales, at about four to six times in two or three minutes, then sound (dive) for as long as twenty minutes. Often they go

A southern right whale surfaces to blow (above);
the spray can be seen from afar on the cold seas.

TUNELESS TALKERS

Whale talk includes some of the eeriest and most beautiful animal sounds. Right whales may not be as eloquent as humpbacks or belugas, but they have a fine repertoire. They can growl or bellow into the air, with the head exposed, or emit low-pitched underwater sounds associated with travel, courtship, and perhaps play. The sounds are rather erratic and coarse; they are mainly moans and belches, produced singly or in short groups, and especially at night.

Studies of the southern right whale have identified several types of sounds: up, down, high, hybrid, pulsive, and constant. For example, "up" calls last about a second, begin low and rise to higher frequencies, and seem to be a contact sign for other whales. "Down" calls swoop from high to low and travel for hundreds of miles, perhaps for long-distance announcements.

straight down and reappear at almost the same spot. They lift their vast heads from the water to see goings-on nearby; they can breach clear of the water and crash in backward. The double blow is even more spectacular than that of the right whale, rising up to 23 ft (7 m) in the icy air. Like right whales, bowheads rarely strand, and they are mostly unafraid of ships, so they can be approached by whale-watchers with a fair degree of confidence.

THE WRIGGLING WHALE

Since it is shy, elusive, and rare, few details are known of the pygmy right whale. As whales go, it has a most unusual method of breathing. There is little or no spout, because this small whale throws its head clear of the water, up and back to breathe, and then sinks under the surface, without showing its dorsal fin or flukes. Most other whales, by contrast, roll forward, exposing their upperparts from nose to flukes, to clear the blowhole. The pygmy right whale breathes every 45–60 seconds and dives for only three or four minutes. Breaching is rare, and cruising speed is low, at only 3 mph (5 km/h).

The pygmy right whale may swim with sei and short-finned pilot whales, which makes its population numbers hard to estimate. It tends to wriggle with a snakelike up-and-down body motion rather than swishing mainly the flukes. ■

There is no mistaking a right whale's high-curved mouth line and heavily encrusted snout.

HABITATS

Right whales are suited to cool and icy oceans in both hemispheres, owing to their preferences for certain foods, which are found only in these areas. Both northern and southern populations are found all the way around the globe at extreme latitudes. Although there is open water between the two populations, it consists of tropical and subtropical seas, where the temperatures, food sources, and other conditions are unsuitable for right whales. So the northern and southern populations are geographically isolated by their habitat preferences.

This situation is not unique to right whales; most of the baleen whales are found in both hemispheres. Most also migrate toward the pole in the summer of their own hemisphere, returning to warmer temperate or subtropical waters during their winter. The right whales follow this general trend, but the seasons are six months out of phase between the hemispheres. So the northern and southern populations seldom, if ever, meet. This geographical isolation can gradually lead to differences in size, color, and other features, which progress through subspecies level until full, separate species status is reached. The northern and southern right whales are somewhere along this continuum.

"THE WHALE"

The northern right whale subspecies (or species) ranges across the North Atlantic and North Pacific. Or at least it did; these whales were once

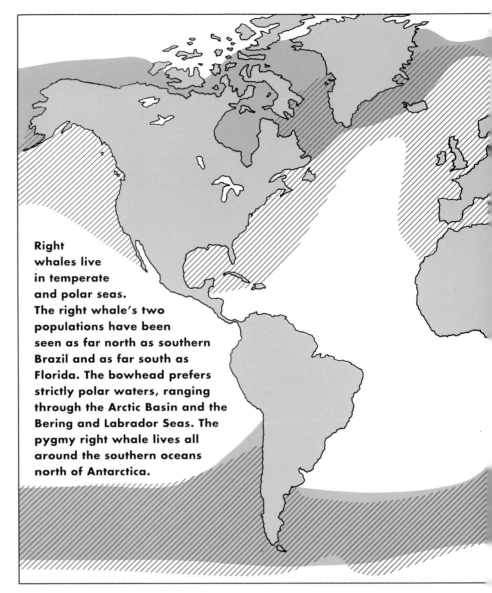

Right whales live in temperate and polar seas. The right whale's two populations have been seen as far north as southern Brazil and as far south as Florida. The bowhead prefers strictly polar waters, ranging through the Arctic Basin and the Bering and Labrador Seas. The pygmy right whale lives all around the southern oceans north of Antarctica.

Des & Jen Bartlett/Survival Anglia

so common, and so visible to humans because they moved so slowly, at the surface, and in coastal areas, that they were simply referred to as "common whales" or "the whales." In ancient Greece, natural historians referred to the right whale as *balaena*, the "true whale," and distinguished it from the blunt-headed, cone-toothed *physeter*, or sperm whale.

Today, after centuries of slaughter, the picture is very different. Northern right whales are scarce, and only remnant groups remain of the once-large populations. In summer they feed in the subarctic and northern temperate waters, but they do not stray to the extreme north, where bowheads live. They spend the months feeding and perhaps later indulge in some courtship and mating behavior, although this may be for social rather than reproductive reasons. By autumn they are on the move to warmer waters in the south of the northern temperate zone.

A southern right whale calf basks with its mother off the Argentine coast (left).

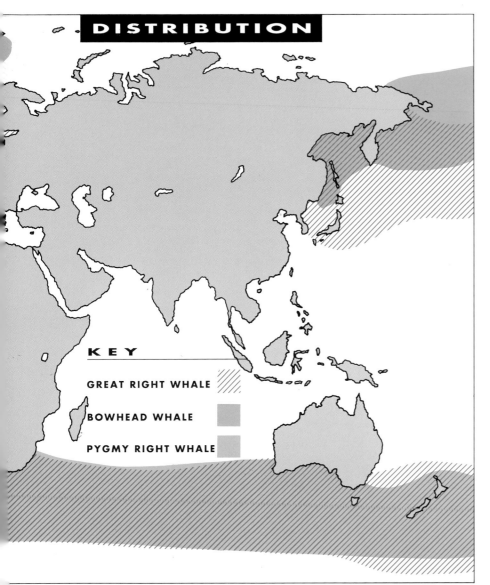

DISTRIBUTION

KEY

GREAT RIGHT WHALE

BOWHEAD WHALE

PYGMY RIGHT WHALE

shrimplike krill that sustain the rorqual baleen whales, such as the blue. But they still have plenty of food in the rich Antarctic Ocean. During their winter, from about May to October, the southern right whales have moved close to the southern coasts of South America, southern Africa, and Australasia.

THE POLAR WHALE

The bowhead is truly a whale of the far northern oceans, frequenting the world's coldest seas, where the temperature is often below freezing. It follows the edge of the pack ice as it retreats in summer and advances again each winter. Bowheads even dive under the floes and sheets, and local people have described them breaking through ice over three feet (about one meter) thick to breathe.

Since the bowhead moves with the edge of the ice, this means it follows a fairly regular migration. It winters in the Arctic and Bering Seas, where the calves are born. The whales then swim northeast in spring, mating as they go, from March to May. As channels or leads appear in the ice, they cruise through to the Beaufort Sea. As they travel, they tend to stay near shorelines, in groups segregated by age and sex. On the return journey, their route is usually farther from the shore, and the groups stick closer together.

BIG AND WARM

Right whales are warm-blooded mammals. Indeed, their body temperatures are similar to ours, about 95–104°F. So how do they survive life in polar waters? The rights and other great whales fit the theory that warm-blooded animals evolve greater

By winter they may have traveled as far south as Florida, Spain, and North Africa, southern Japan, and northern California.

The summer quarters of the main surviving populations of northern right whales comprise four main areas: between Asia and North America, in the Bering, Chukchi, Beaufort, and Siberian seas; in the Davis Strait, Baffin Bay, and Hudson Bay of northern North America; in the Sea of Okhotsk in the western Pacific, north of Japan; and possibly in the northeast Atlantic north of Scandinavia, around Svalbard, although this group is close to extinction.

IN THE ANTARCTIC

Southern right whales live between latitudes of about 20°S and 50°S, so they are rarely found in the Antarctic Circle. This means they do not venture far enough south to feed on the rich swarms of

Right whales live in flexible groups, meeting up or dispersing as seasons and food supplies change.

François Gohier/Ardea

size in more extreme climates—in this case, cold ones. The reasoning is concerned with body volume compared to body surface area. The larger the animal, the smaller its surface area per unit of body volume. This means it has proportionally less surface area through which to lose heat, so it can use less food energy to stay warm. The right whales also have thick layers of oily and fatty blubber just under the skin, which provide excellent insulation and help minimize heat loss.

There are also heat-exchange mechanisms at the bases of the flippers and flukes. Arteries taking blood into the extremities run alongside veins that bring it back to the heart. The warm blood in the arteries donates some of its heat to the cooled blood. This means the extremity is a few degrees cooler than the main body, though still warm enough to function, and this reduces heat loss from it, while the body's inner or core temperature remains high.

A SOUTHERN SWIMMER

The pygmy right whale is found only in the southern oceans, north of Antarctica, in more temperate zones. It has been spotted both inshore and far out at sea, and in most parts of its range at most times of the year. This means its migrations are probably more diffuse than those of its larger cousins. ∎

François Gohier/Ardea

FOCUS ON

CAPE COD

Cape Cod, southeast of Boston, is one of the United State's premier tourist areas. Because it benefits from the Gulf Stream currents, it has a temperate continental climate, with warm, moist summers and cold, damp winters. The Cape curls out from the coast like a big fishhook, extending 65 miles (105 km) into the North Atlantic and encircling Cape Cod Bay. In 1914, the Cape was severed at its base from the mainland by the Cape Cod Canal, a 17.5-mile (28-km) shipping lane. From the time of the early European settlers in the 17th century, the Cape has been a base for fishing; indeed, it was named after the teeming codfish in the surrounding waters. It was also a whaling port.

About 350 northern right whales still frequent Cape Cod for breeding in winter and spring. They are a valued attraction for sailors and whale-watchers. Other local attractions include the Cape Cod National Seashore, an area of sand dunes, pinewoods, and marshes covering some 68 sq miles (175 sq km) of the northern shore.

WHY MIGRATE?

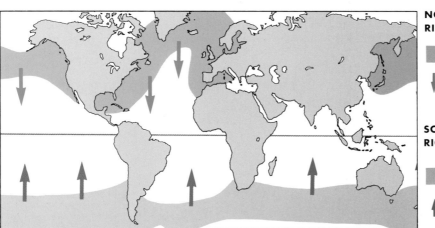

NORTHERN RIGHT WHALE

■ RANGE

↓ MIGRATION

SOUTHERN RIGHT WHALE

■ RANGE

↑ MIGRATION

In the polar waters, the long daylight hours and abundant nutrients cause a summer flush of food. But in winter, these areas are too cold and dark for food, or for giving birth. So the whales head toward the temperate and subtropical waters to rest and calve. Because the northern winter coincides with the southern summer, the migrations of the two different right whale populations are staggered by six months.

NEIGHBORS

The waters of Cape Cod are unusually warm for the region because they are fed by the Gulf Stream currents. They are full of crustaceans and fish, which attract flocks of seabirds.

ATLANTIC SALMON

Salmon are born far inland. Years later they migrate to the sea, then return to their home river to spawn.

COMMON EIDER

This big Arctic sea duck breeds on northern coasts, flying over pods of right whales and bowheads.

Neighbor illustrations Joanne Cowne

CAPE COD

Cape Cod lies southeast of Boston, Massachusetts, some 250 miles (400 km) up the eastern U.S. coast from New York City. Tapering dramatically to its extreme point, the Cape ranges in breadth from 1 to 20 miles (1.6 to 32 km). To its south lie the islands of Nantucket and Martha's Vineyard, and to its north stretches the Gulf of Maine.

CANADA
UNITED STATES
BOSTON
CAPE COD
NEW YORK
North Atlantic

CLAMS

Clams filter food from the seawater and hide in the muddy bed of coastal waters.

LEATHERBACK

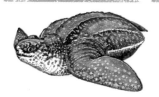

The huge leatherback can be found in temperate seas, where right whales come to spend winter.

GLAUCOUS GULL

These large gulls dwell along the Arctic coasts of North America and Europe, flying south in winter.

KITTIWAKE

This seabird nests in huge colonies on the ledges of island cliffs. It snatches fish from the surface waters.

COD

Cod are found across the Atlantic to the Bay of Biscay. They eat worms, crustaceans, and fish.

FOOD AND FEEDING

Right and bowhead whales are filter-feeders. They cruise continuously through their food, which is suspended in the water, without pausing to gulp in mouthfuls like other rorquals. This feeding technique produces huge pressures and strains on the whale's head and body. Imagine, for example, trying to tow a car through the water with its hood open. This is why the whales swim slowly and have the biggest head and shortest neck of almost any mammal. The jaws and skull are specially shaped and jointed with ligaments and huge muscles.

COPEPODS AND KRILL

Right whales feed on two main kinds of food items: copepods and krill. Copepods are small crustaceans with a flattened body casing. There are many different species; taken together, copepods are probably the most numerous creatures on the planet. Krill are closely related to the true shrimps and prawns; they range from the size of a finger down to that of a maggot. Both copepods and krill are easy to eat because they tend to occur in dense swarms. The southern right whale feeds on *Calanus* species of copepods and *Euphausia* krill. The northern ones eat *Calanus* copepods, *Meganyctiphanis* krill—adults and larvae—and various other crustaceans.

The secret of the right whales' filter-feeding lies in their baleen. There are 225–250 light gray baleen plates

Illustration Kim Thompson

on each side of the jaw. Their inner edges fray into fine, silky fibers like an old rug and form a huge, fine-mesh sieve on either side of the mouth, which can strain out copepods only one inch long.

When feeding, the right whale swims slowly near the surface, holding its mouth open at an angle of 10–15° and with only the tip showing above the surface. The water flows through the baleen at a rate of 530 cubic feet (15 cubic meters) per minute, and the plates may make a rattling sound. The trapped food is scraped from the baleen and pushed into the throat by the rasping tongue. Occasionally the whale inclines its head to change the water flow and swish the baleen clean, since such fine sieves clog easily.

The right whale may use the same technique but dives to midwater, about 30 ft (10 m) down, and stays under for up to ten minutes. If the water contains floating debris such as seaweed, the whale stops frequently to clean its baleen, rolling the weed into a ball with its tongue and flicking it away.

Right whales have also been seen to stand on their heads on the seabed, feeding on bottom-dwelling shellfish, though it is not known if this is an important part of their diet. They also "accidentally" consume a variety of other creatures, including fish, jellyfish, and even small seabirds, due to their rather nonselective method of sifting the sea.

During their early development, baleen whales actually have typical mammal teeth. These degenerate, however, and the baleen plates (right) *grow from another structure in the roof of the mouth.*

TRAWLING

The bowhead is a surface feeder, slowly cruising along with its mouth agape. Water is forced into the front of its mouth and out the sides; on the way it is strained through the long, fine curtains of baleen, which sieve out copepods and other crustaceans (below).

Des & Jen Bartlett/Bruce Coleman Ltd.

KEY FACTS

● **The bowhead and right whale probably eat between 1.1 and 2.8 tons of food each day; the pygmy right whale may need 110–220 lb (50–100 kg) of food daily.**

● **Humans probably eat about 3.3 lb (1.5 kg) of food each day. This may not sound like much—but at least we eat every day. Right whales eat a great deal in summer, but very little during their winter season, while they are giving birth. Then they may consume almost no food for up to five months.**

The bowhead's baleen is even more impressive. There are 325–360 baleen plates on each side of the jaw, and in a large individual the longest plates may be over 13 ft (4 m), by far the longest of any great whale. The jaw is held open wider than in the right whale, at up to 50°. A bowhead skim-feeds in much the same way as a right whale; sometimes it swims along on its side, mouth gaping. It has also been known to stir the seabed up to 200 ft (60 m) down and sieve the sediment as it surfaces, like a gray whale. Another technique is water-column feeding—diving and swimming back up vertically, sieving as it rises, for up to 20 minutes. As many as 30 whales may do this together. In general, when food is abundant they feed together, but when it is scarce they separate. The size of their feeding groups vary according to the food availablity.

PRIMITIVE PYGMIES

The stomach contents of caught pygmy right whales show that they feed on copepods such as the *Calanus* species. There are about 220 whitish baleen plates up to 28 in (70 cm) long in either side of the jaw, and it is presumed that these whales filter-feed like their bigger relatives, but the detailed feeding techniques are not known. The presence of two throat grooves or pleats may allow for throat expansion and indicate that pygmy rights gulp-feed for some of the time. These throat grooves are only rudimentary in the primitive pygmy right whale, as opposed to those of the rorquals. ■

SOCIAL STRUCTURE

Right whales and bowheads are both solitary and social. They are sometimes observed alone, sometimes in loose groups, and also in more tight-knit groups. Today their social behavior is conducted under very changed circumstances, since they are now so rare. It is likely that right whales are basically social animals, and that when they were more numerous they formed groups of up to a hundred animals.

The basic right whale social unit seems to be two to ten animals. Individuals come and go, swimming alone or within a mile or so of another group for hours, then rejoining or leaving to find a new group. The groups also merge and separate frequently, and the only enduring relationship seems to be that between a mother and her calf.

When the calf is about four months old, the mother and calf become very close. They begin to swim as fast as they can, up and down the coastline, in preparation for their migration. The closeness of the pair helps protect the youngster on migration

from attacks by killer whales and sharks, and from storms that could separate the calf from its mother.

Mother and young spend about six months at the summer feeding area. During this time the youngster becomes more independent, although it still takes milk. When the pair returns to the calving grounds, the mother distances herself from her calf, although the calf may still approach her and try to close the gap. Eventually she leaves, and the calf joins a playful group of other youngsters and young adults. They splash their flippers and leap and breach, often many times in succession. They begin to show more adult communication signals, such as an exaggerated blow, which indicates irritation, and slapping flippers or flukes onto the surface to show excitement or aggression.

SONGS BENEATH THE SEA

Right whales seem to keep in contact even over long distances with various calls. When dispersed, they produce low-frequency sounds that travel well. As

SPY-HOPPING

The right whale raises its head to watch and listen briefly (below). *In this way it can detect enemies, such as killer whales, and also spot its fellows. It may also look for landmarks on its migration routes.*

 SIGHT

BOWHEAD SONGS

Several types of bowhead calls have been detected. One of these is a medium moan, compared to a trombone sliding up and down the scale and lasting up to five seconds. Others include a low purring sound consisting of about fifty pulses per second for up to three seconds, a higher and more variable purr like an ecstatic cat, and a stop-start purr or buzz.

Currently, however, little is known about the purpose of these calls. As with other whales, their meaning will probably become clearer in time. It is not even known how baleens utter sound; it is easy enough for us to make a noise, since we can breathe in afterward, but whales obviously cannot do so. Humpbacks avoid exhaling by recycling the air that they force through the larynx. In doing so, they can "sing" for half an hour or longer.

Robin Budden/Wildlife Art Agency

LOB-TAILING

Right whales often breach and lob-tail, or tail-slap, during courtship. The whale comes to the surface, tips its head down, and raises its flukes into the air, then it slaps them on the surface (below right). This may be one method of indicating its position to others, or it could simply be a display of sheer exuberance.

they come together, they emit more high-pitched sounds, which increase as the size of the social group increases. This may reflect increased excitement levels associated with sexual behavior.

The sounds termed hybrid calls—a mixture of pitches and volumes—indicate increased aggression among males, especially at breeding time. So do pulsive calls, which to our ears resemble harsh growls or groans. When an intimidated whale leaves its rivals, they make excited, high-pitched, almost melodic noises, as though in triumph.

BOWHEADS IN FORMATION

Bowhead whales usually swim alone or in groups of up to three or four. Like the right whale, these whales are fundamentally social. In the days when they were more common, they were able to follow their natural instincts and gather in aggregations of a hundred or more.

The density of the krill and copepods has a marked effect on bowhead grouping behavior. Where the food is adequate but not plentiful, they

tend to feed alone. In dense, plentiful swarms of food, they may skim-feed and swim together. In some cases there are up to fifteen animals, and they travel in a V formation, with a lead animal or two, and others in a staggered diagonal line on each side—similar to a migrating flock of geese.

And like their right whale relatives, young bowheads exhibit play behavior. During the summer feeding season, the calves may be left alone for up to half an hour while the mothers dive to feed. During this time, mother and young keep in touch with calls that rise and fall in pitch, and the youngsters often find an object to play with. Logs and other driftwood are favorites; the calf swims toward the log, ducks under it, lays alongside it, and noses it about. Youngsters and adults have also been seen to flick or toss drifting logs, push them under so that they bob back up again, and even balance them on their backs and let them roll off with a splash. As with young mammals on land, this play probably helps the youngsters to practice their defense techniques. ■

REPRODUCTION

Instead of forming firm pair bonds, right whales are promiscuous: Each mature male tries to mate as many times as he can, with as many females as possible. The competition between males to father young has shifted from battling rivals before mating, as in many mammals, to producing bigger quantities of sperm-containing seminal fluid than the rivals. The intention is that this huge volume of sperm—more than 13 gallons (50 liters)—displaces any other sperm from the female's reproductive tract, possibly turning its producer into the father.

At mating time, a receptive female right whale is surrounded by up to six males. Males often have more scars on their bodies, indicating that they may push or butt each other and cause wounds with their hard callosities. Courtship includes breaching, pushing and nuzzling, stroking with the flippers, and caressing with the flukes. The males slap the water agitatedly with their flippers and tails. The female dives and circles, the males following in courtship ritual. If she is unreceptive she may lie on the seabed, or on her back at the surface, so the males cannot reach her.

THE MATING TRIAD

The breeding congregation may well resolve into a triad, where one male supports the female from below while another copulates with her. This may not be cooperation but competition, since the female is jostled by several males trying to mate with her.

In both northern and southern right whales, the mating time is usually late winter or early spring in the respective hemispheres. It tends to occur in

GROWING UP

The life of a young right whale

MATING TRIAD
*While a pair mates
(below), a second male
supports the female
from beneath her.*

LEARNING THE BASICS
*While very young, a right whale calf constantly
alternates between breathing at the surface and
diving to suckle from its mother (below).*

Howard Hall/Oxford Scientific Films

deeper water, away from the coast, as the whales head off on their migration to the summer feeding grounds. With a gestation period of nine or ten months, this means that calves are born the following winter, after the return to warmer waters. In the north, the peak calving time is November to January; in the south around Africa and Australia, May to July; and a month or two later off South America. The pregnant females collect in shallow, sheltered bays, sometimes within a stone's throw of the shore.

The typical right whale female produces a single baby every three years: pregnant for ten months,

*Fed exclusively on its mother's rich milk for at
least a year, the right whale calf grows rapidly.*

feeding the baby for fourteen months, and resting and feeding herself for twelve months.

Moments after birth, the mother pushes the baby to the surface to breathe. Its tail is curved and weak at first from being folded inside the womb. It soon strengthens, and the calf can swim within a few hours. Right whale young spend a considerable amount of time playing. Each mother and baby stay in the shallow, calm, protected water of the birthing bay for about four months. During this time the calf learns to surface and breathe, swim and dive smoothly, and to practice filter-feeding.

At first, the calf stays right next to its mother for protection from predators, and the two touch each other constantly. The youngster throws up its head to breathe, then dives under her belly to feed on her milk. Her nipples are hidden inside mammary folds of skin. Whale milk is extremely rich in fat—40 percent or more per volume—to give the youngster plenty of energy and to build up its blubbery insulation. As the first month passes, the baby begins to swim farther from its mother, and it practices circling, rolling, lying on its back, breaching, and other maneuvers. Some calves leap from the water in exuberant fashion every minute for up to an hour.

Most great whales reach sexual maturity at a certain size, not a certain age. In some whale species, especially the rorquals, the dramatically reduced numbers due to whaling has led to the whales' growing faster, and therefore reaching sexual

Ralph & Daphne Keller/NHPA

A mother and calf frolic in the warm seas, observed by another adult (above).

PLAYING WITH MOTHER
As it gains confidence, the calf becomes playful, rolling and diving around its tolerant mother (above left).

maturity younger. This may be partly because there is more food available. However, it is not clear if right whales have responded in this way.

The bowhead breeds in much the same way as the right whale, although the males are less promiscuous and more aggressive to rivals. Like the rights, they mate belly to belly, standing vertically in the water with the tips of the snouts and chins exposed. Mating usually takes place in spring, on the northward migration. Babies are born early the next spring in wintering areas such as the Bering Sea.

Very little is known about the pygmy right whale's breeding season behavior. It seems that young are born in early spring, around September or October, although some reports say that these whales can mate or give birth at almost any time of the year. ■

in SIGHT

HOW OLD ARE RIGHT WHALES?

Right and bowhead whales were almost wiped out before people devised modern scientific methods of telling their age. One method is to examine the waxy earplug that stops up the outer ear of the whale, preventing water from entering. As the whale grows, the plug gets bigger by adding layers. Coupled with studies of other, better known whales, this gives a rough longevity for right whales of fifty years, although some scientists believe they may live up to seventy years.

FROM BIRTH TO DEATH

RIGHT WHALE
GESTATION: 9–12 MONTHS
NO. OF YOUNG: 1
LENGTH AT BIRTH: 16 FT (5 M)
WEIGHT AT BIRTH: 5.5 TONS
WEANING: 12–14 MONTHS
INDEPENDENCE: 2–3 YEARS
SEXUAL MATURITY: MALE 5–12 YEARS, FEMALE PROBABLY EARLIER
LONGEVITY: 50–70 YEARS

BOWHEAD WHALE
GESTATION: 10–11 MONTHS
NO. OF YOUNG: 1, SOMETIMES 2
LENGTH AT BIRTH: 13 FT (4 M)
WEIGHT AT BIRTH: 4.4–5.5 TONS
WEANING: 6–10 MONTHS
INDEPENDENCE: 2 YEARS
SEXUAL MATURITY: PROBABLY SIMILAR TO RIGHT WHALE
LONGEVITY: NOT KNOWN

PYGMY RIGHT WHALE
GESTATION: 10–11 MONTHS
LITTER SIZE: 1
LENGTH AT BIRTH: 5–6.5 FT (1.5–2 M)
WEIGHT AT BIRTH: 1,100 LB (500 KG)
WEANING: WHEN CALF IS 11.5 FT

(3.5 M) LONG. PROBABLY AT LEAST 1 YEAR OLD
SEXUAL MATURITY: NOT KNOWN
LONGEVITY: NOT KNOWN, POSSIBLY 30 YEARS

THE IDEAL VICTIMS

IT DID NOT TAKE WHALERS LONG TO REALIZE THAT RIGHT WHALES HAD ALL THE QUALITIES DESIRED IN A VICTIM OF THE HARPOON—SO THESE UNLUCKY, TRUSTING CREATURES CRUISED SLOWLY INTO DEEP TROUBLE

Right whales have always been under threat; it is part of nature. They are preyed on by sharks and toothed whales. They suffer from parasites such as lice and intestinal worms. They become sick and develop cancers, stomach ulcers, weak hearts, respiratory infections such as pneumonia, blood conditions such as jaundice, and osteoarthritis and other joint problems. All of these become more common and threatening with increasing age.

But right whales also had qualities that made them especially attractive to whalers. Their blubber, thicker than in other baleens, gave a high oil yield and helped them float when dead. The silky baleen was long and fine and especially prized. Right whales were hunted for centuries before any other species became commercial targets. Their numbers were already critically low by the time mechanized whaling took off in the last century. Today, right whales are still very rare, and just hanging on—maybe even recovering—from the slaughter.

EASY MEAT

The killing of right whales began more than seven centuries ago. Many species of whales have been used and consumed by humans for thousands of years, especially along the coasts of North America and northern Asia. These people hunted only small numbers of whales, or took advantage of beached individuals. The new threat was the organized hunting of whales in large numbers by skilled sailors in seagoing vessels—and the right whales were their primary targets.

The breeding haunts and migration routes of the right whales took them regularly into coastal waters. A favorite calving place for northern right whales in the eastern Atlantic was the Bay of Biscay, off western France and northern Spain, where the deep water runs close to the shore. The local people, the

Basques, took the occasional beached whale. They used the oil and blubber for fuel, the skin for garments, the meat for food, and the baleen and bones for carvings and implements. They realized that the whales could be forcibly beached by throwing spears at them from boats to their seaward side.

From this, it was but a short step to tackling the whales in the water with spears and axes. One of the right whale's "right" qualities is that when dead, it still floats—unlike many other whales, which must be inflated with air to keep them at the surface. The carcasses were floated to shore to be cut up. This gave plenty of fresh meat and other by-products.

The Basques built tall watchtowers and manned clifftop viewpoints along the coasts to look for the whales. By the 12th century, the villagers of the Biscay coast were coming to depend on a

Tui de Roy/Oxford Scientific Films

Locals try to rescue a pygmy right whale stranded on a South American beach (above).

Steve McCucheon/Frank Lane Picture Agency

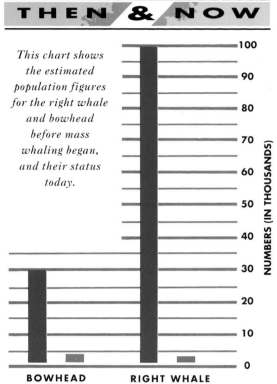

THEN & NOW

This chart shows the estimated population figures for the right whale and bowhead before mass whaling began, and their status today.

NUMBERS (IN THOUSANDS)

100
90
80
70
60
50
40
30
20
10
0

BOWHEAD   RIGHT WHALE

■ POPULATION BEFORE MASS WHALING
(ABOUT A.D. 1200)

■ POPULATION TODAY

These numbers are very approximate; cetaceans are notoriously difficult to count, even if the species can be told apart in a mixed herd from glimpses as they surface to blow. Some authorities say that a large proportion of double-counting is almost inevitable, and the true numbers may be less than those shown above. There is certainly no room for complacency.

thriving whaling industry. They included scenes of whaling in their coats of arms and received hunting grants from the king. The main weapon they used was the spearlike *arpoi*, which became the harpoon. The boat they used was a *chaloupe*, which became the shallop—the vessel used by more recent South Sea whalers.

FISHED OUT

Perhaps as early as the 14th century, adventurous Basque whaling ships were sailing farther afield, perhaps to the Gulf of St. Lawrence—far in advance of the main European discoverers—and to Iceland.

What a waste: This right whale was too heavy for local North Americans to haul out onto shore.

(in)SIGHT

ALASKAN HUNTERS

The United State's 1972 Marine Mammal Protection Act prohibited commercial whaling in U.S. seas, except for subsistence and traditional uses by native people such as the Inuit, Aleuts, Amerindians, and Alaskans.

Alaskan people have hunted bowheads for centuries. Traditionally, they use large boats made of a wooden frame covered with walrus hide. The bowhead's migration routes through the cracks in the ice make them easy to catch.

Before European and American whalers decimated the bowhead's populations, these subsistence hunts had little effect on whale numbers. Bowheads and right whales were protected from 1936, but the people of the far north were allowed to continue their traditional pursuit. But their quotas of 20–30 bowheads per year, coupled with natural whale mortalities, may now be a significant threat to the species.

The traditional hunt may have to stop if the whales are to survive. One suggestion is that the Eskimos hunt gray whales instead.

By the 16th century, most of the right whales in the Bay of Biscay area had been "fished out"—a colloquial but inapt phrase, since whales are of course mammals. Naturally, the Basques wished to continue their business and use their traditional skills. So they built even larger ships and followed their quarry even farther, northwest across the Atlantic on the migration routes as far as Newfoundland.

By this time, Dutch sailors had also discovered the riches of whaling in the North Atlantic. The first English expedition took place in 1610, and several other European countries soon followed. Many of the Basques, with their long-standing experience of whaling, took on the role of paid consultants on these expeditions.

Right whales were becoming rarer, and countries vied for the remaining populations. While the rest of 17th-century Europe argued about whaling rights, in the 1620s the Dutch built Smeerenburg, or "Blubber Town," on the Spitsbergen archipelago in Norway. It was a perfect land base for processing right and bowhead whales that were fat from the rich feeding of their far-northern summer feeding grounds. At the peak of the industry, 18,000 men and 300 whaling ships were based at the port.

François Gohier/Ardea

ENDANGERED SPECIES

WRONGING THE RIGHTS

In 1931, the League of Nations (the interwar forerunner of the United Nations) drafted a convention to regulate whaling that was due to come into force in 1935. Right and bowhead whales were on the protected list, and in theory, hunting them was illegal from 1936. But in practice, not all countries were in the League of Nations, some of those that were did not adhere to the convention, and World War II soon overshadowed all such events.

There are other hazards facing the bowhead and right whales. When the population of any animal reaches such low numbers, events that might be absorbed or dissipated by a larger population assume much greater significance. These include inbreeding due to a lack of unrelated mates among the survivors. A disease epidemic might obliterate the population before members have time to develop immunity to it. There are also increasing levels of pollution along the west and east coasts of the North Atlantic, including heavy metals and organic toxins. In addition, right whales may be at risk when they come inshore to calve or shelter, as at Cape Cod. And there is the simple, mathematically reduced chance of finding a mate at all in the wide ocean.

Even after sixty years of theoretical full protection, the right and bowhead whales

CONSERVATION MEASURES

The following protection measures exist for whales in general:

● Legal protection from 1936

● Full legal protection again in the 1940s by the International Whaling Commission

● Banning of commercial whaling in the waters of various nations from the 1970s

remain extremely vulnerable. Some of the rorquals, such as the humpback, seem to be increasing their populations, partly as a result of young whales maturing earlier and beginning to breed more quickly. However, these trends are not apparent in the right whale.

Part of the answer may be in the "new ecology" of the oceans. As the right and then the rorqual whales were slaughtered, the copepods and krill that they would have eaten became available to other animals. These have not been slow to take advantage. Various species of fish, squid, and seabirds have been exploiting the spare food, and humans have begun to harvest krill. So even if the right whales have the numbers and the genetic diversity to increase, the food resources may simply not be there any more to help them fight their way back.

Inset photograph Des & Jen Bartlett/Survival Anglia

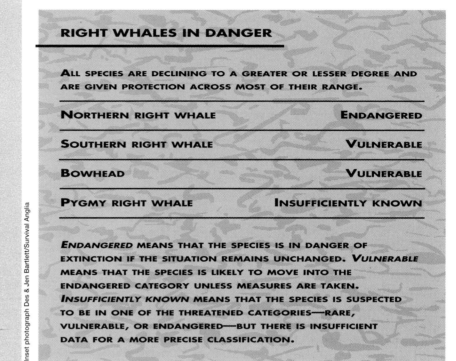

RIGHT WHALES IN DANGER

ALL SPECIES ARE DECLINING TO A GREATER OR LESSER DEGREE AND ARE GIVEN PROTECTION ACROSS MOST OF THEIR RANGE.

NORTHERN RIGHT WHALE	ENDANGERED
SOUTHERN RIGHT WHALE	VULNERABLE
BOWHEAD	VULNERABLE
PYGMY RIGHT WHALE	INSUFFICIENTLY KNOWN

ENDANGERED MEANS THAT THE SPECIES IS IN DANGER OF EXTINCTION IF THE SITUATION REMAINS UNCHANGED. *VULNERABLE* MEANS THAT THE SPECIES IS LIKELY TO MOVE INTO THE ENDANGERED CATEGORY UNLESS MEASURES ARE TAKEN. *INSUFFICIENTLY KNOWN* MEANS THAT THE SPECIES IS SUSPECTED TO BE IN ONE OF THE THREATENED CATEGORIES—RARE, VULNERABLE, OR ENDANGERED—BUT THERE IS INSUFFICIENT DATA FOR A MORE PRECISE CLASSIFICATION.

AN INQUISITIVE BUT CAUTIOUS CREW ARE DWARFED BY A SOUTHERN RIGHT WHALE AND HER CALF.

● Strict control on international trade in whale products under CITES terms from the 1970s

● A worldwide moratorium on commercial whaling of large cetacean species from 1986

● Establishment of refuges, such as the Southern Ocean Refuge in 1994, and special protection for the remaining inshore calving grounds

As North America was colonized by Europeans, a new whaling industry developed in the northwest Atlantic. The early fleets sailed in the 1690s to catch migrating right whales off Long Island. The industry spread along the coast, and whaling ships also began to patrol the edges of the Arctic pack ice and hunt bowheads in larger numbers. The large boats took processing equipment such as tryworks (brick ovens for rendering blubber) with them. Some voyages lasted over four years, and the conditions were infamously hard and dirty. But with luck and skill, a whaler would return to port with its oil barrels full, making its crew members wealthy men.

DOWN SOUTH

By the early 1700s, right whales had become extremely scarce all around the coasts of the north and mid-Atlantic. The whalers set about killing bowheads in even greater numbers. In about 1712, New England whalers discovered that they could also kill sperm whales (which also floated when dead) far out at sea, and tow them back to shore, for even greater financial rewards. The spotlight of North Atlantic whaling turned away from the rights and bowheads. But it was, in effect, already too late. The right and bowhead whales had been all but wiped out and were no longer an economical target.

The southern right whales suffered a similar fate, but it happened with astonishing speed. There was some whaling in the South Atlantic and South Pacific during the late 18th century, and whaling bases were set up along the coast of southern South America and nearby islands. In the 1830s, whalers discovered large numbers of southern right whales in the southeast Pacific, off South America. They were again easy targets, since they came even closer to the coast to breed than their northern cousins. Between 1835 and 1839, a total of about 12,000 southern right whales where taken. During the following six years, the number taken fell to 7,000. By 1850, the numbers were so low that right whaling operations in the south almost ceased.

FARTHER NORTH

Other whaling fleets pursued the remaining northern rights and bowheads even farther north, along the northern coasts of Asia and North America and around the Bering Sea, risking intense cold and being trapped and crushed by advancing ice. The bowhead, being the largest right whale with the longest baleen and highest oil yield, became the new prize. It had been hunted around Svalbard from the 1700s, until stocks were exhausted. Then bowheads were pursued off Greenland, Baffin Island, Hudson Bay, and finally into the North Pacific, around the Bering and Okhotsk Seas. But it was virtually all over for the right whales and bowheads. Of the many tens of thousands in prewhaling days, only a few hundred survived.

And so the situation remained during the late 19th and early 20th centuries, as modern mass whaling developed. The easy targets of right whales

ALONGSIDE MAN

THE RIGHT STUFF

Each right or bowhead whale yielded up to 100 barrels—over 2,600 gallons (10,000 liters)—of oil. This was used as fuel for lamps and in cooking, as a lubricant, for leather tanning, and in soap and paint manufacture.

The right whale's baleen—1,550 lb (700 kg) from each whale—was the finest and longest of all whalebone whales. It was made into umbrella ribs, fishing rods, carriage springs, whips, and supporting garments such as the farthingale skirt of Elizabethan times, the 19th-century hooped skirt, and Victorian corsets or whalebone stays. The finer inner fibers were woven into stiff fabrics such as taffeta and crinoline.

Whale cartilages and bones were used to produce glues or ground up for fertilizer. "Scrimshaw" is the art of carving or engraving on whalebone, as well as on the tusks of walruses, narwhals, and elephants, and the teeth of toothed whales. It began in the 1820s as a way of passing time on whaling ships, but few right whales were caught after this time.

Their trusting nature once doomed the right whales. Now, humans approach them with peaceful intentions.

and bowheads were gone. The rorquals such as the blue and fin whales were faster, but more wary, prey. So whalers used explosive harpoons, engine-powered catcher boats, and huge factory ships. Inevitably, within a century, the rorquals had gone much the same way as their right whale cousins.

PROTECTION AT LAST

Despite their desperately low numbers, right and bowhead whales were almost ignored as endangered species and were not officially protected until 1936. As a new awareness of the horrors of whaling has developed over the past thirty years, right whales have tended to tag along behind their more high-profile cousins such as the blue and sperm whales, but they are equally in need of protection.

The International Whaling Commission (IWC) was set up in 1946 to regulate the industry, and, in theory, to plan for the future. It gradually introduced lists of protected species, beginning with the right and bowhead whales. It also demarcated refuge areas of sea and when the seasons for whaling were opened or closed.

From the 1950s, the general public became more aware that whales were mammals with complex behavior, that they protected their young, and felt pain as the harpoons hit. Save the Whale campaigns grabbed the headlines. The World Wide Fund for Nature (WWF), Greenpeace, and Friends of the Earth took up the cause. In 1970, the United States banned the import of whale products, and two years later it banned commercial whaling in its territorial waters; most other nations have since followed suit. ■

Doug Allen/Oxford Scientific Films

INTO THE FUTURE

The IWC phased out all commercial whaling by the end of the 1985 season. The moratorium is still in place, although there are increasing moves to end it as far as some of the smaller rorquals are concerned, especially minke whales. Japan, Norway, Iceland, and other nations with great whaling traditions regularly suggest the resumption of killing minkes. The bowhead and right whales, however, are likely to stay protected. CITES (the Convention on International Trade in Endangered Species) has also stemmed the trade in whale products, although there are still black-market economies in some whale meats.

In April–May 1994 the IWC declared a vast ocean sanctuary around Antarctica where all whaling, scientific and commercial, would be prohibited. The boundary follows the 40°S latitude, except near Chile where it dips to 60°S, and in part of the Indian Ocean where it dips to 55°S, to take into account an existing sanctuary north of this line.

PREDICTION

WILL THEY RECOVER?

Hopefully, but it will take a long time. Experts are concerned that, after 60 years of protection, the recovery is too slow, if present at all. Right whales are practically on the increase; bowheads are out of the immediately critical area, but they remain vulnerable, for example to outbreaks of disease.

This refuge includes large areas where the southern right whale spends its summer stocking up on food, which is stored as fat and oil to see it through the leaner winter months. In fact, the sanctuary is thought to be the main feeding area for about three-quarters of the world's remaining great whales. It is hoped that all nations will respect the agreement, which will be reviewed every decade.

The pygmy right whale may not be in immediate danger. Since it sometimes swims with mixed herds of other rorquals, and it has never been of much interest to whalers, its numbers may have been underestimated. Possibly it has always been a fairly scarce species and remains little affected by the centuries of commercial exploitation. ■

WHALE-WATCHING

Whale-watching from cliffs and boats, and even whale-touching with the more curious and gentle cetacean species, is a rapidly growing business. The trend began commercially in the mid-1950s. By 1994, some thirty-five countries had organized whale-watching, with more than five million people taking part. Whale-watching enthusiasts say that the activity is educational, scientific, recreational, and, of course, pleasurable.

In many ways, right whales are the "right" species for this activity. They are usually docile and calm, highly visible at the surface, and big enough to inspire awe in observers. Their preference for regular calving areas means their traveling patterns are predictable to guarantee viewing satisfaction. However, their extreme rarity makes any interference undesirable. Also, they are not as active as the flipper-waving, fluke-smacking, singing-and-dancing species such as the humpback.

STRANDINGS

Nobody is quite sure why whales strand. The most notorious whale for stranding is the pilot whale; massed groups of pilots beach themselves in Newfoundland and Nova Scotia toward autumn. It may be because they are following schools of migrating squid, which throng in the shallow and treacherous coastal waters. Squid are a crucial food source for the pilot whales at this time of year. Another possibility is that whales navigate by Earth's geomagnetic field and stick resolutely to magnetic patterns even when these pass over sandbanks or reefs.

Compared to other cetaceans, right whales rarely strand. These long-lived animals become familiar with the coastlines of their habitual migrations, and the youngsters stay close to their mothers for at least the first year to learn the lay of the land—or seabed. Right whales and bowheads that do strand have usually died from parasitism or sickness and were washed ashore by winds and currents.

Illustration Steve Kingston

Published by Marshall Cavendish Corporation
99 White Plains Road
Tarrytown, New York 10591-9001

© Marshall Cavendish Corporation, 1997
© Marshall Cavendish Ltd, 1994

The material in this series was first published in the English language by Marshall Cavendish Limited, of 119 Wardour Street, London W1V 3TD, England.

Library of Congress Cataloging-in-Publication Data

Encyclopedia of mammals.
    p. cm.
    Includes index.
    ISBN 0-7614-0575-5 (set)   ISBN 0-7614-0590-9 (v. 15)

    Summary: Detailed articles cover the history, anatomy, feeding habits, social structure, reproduction, territory, and current status of ninety-five mammals around the world.
    1. Mammals—Encyclopedias, Juvenile. [l. Mammals—Encyclopedias.] I. Marshall Cavendish Corporation.
    QL706.2.E54 1996
    599'.003—dc20
                                                96-17736
                                                CIP
                                                AC

Printed in Malaysia
Bound in U.S.A.